SPOTLIGHT

MASSACHUSETTS BIKING

CHRIS BERNARD

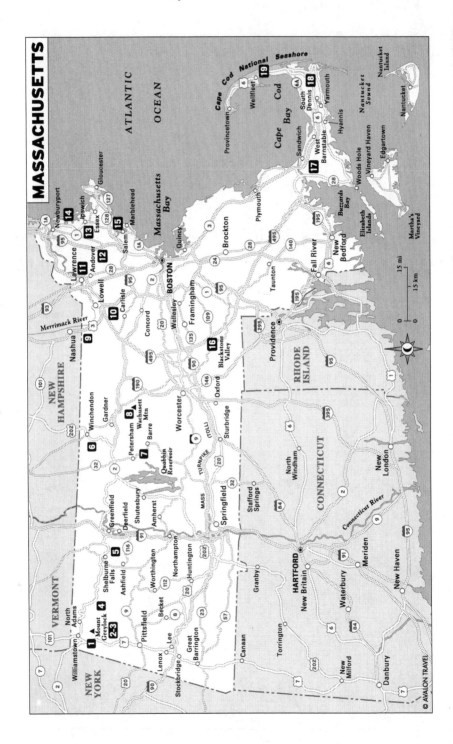

How to Use This Book

ABOUT THE MAPS

Each chapter begins with a region map that shows the locations and numbers of the rides listed in that chapter. Each ride profile is also accompanied by a detailed map that shows the bike route.

Map Symbols

———————	Road Route	o	City
········	Unpaved Road Route	o	Town
------	Trail Route	℗	Trailhead Parking
▰▰ ▰ ▰▰ ▰	Optional Route	Start	Start of Ride
··············	Trail	▪	Point of Interest
·············	Trail (Bikes Prohibited)	★	Natural Feature
▱▱▱▱	Divided Highway	▲	Mountain
▱▱▱	Primary Road	⚑	State Park
▱▱▱▱	Secondary Road	⛰	Campground
▱ ▱ ▱ ▱	Unpaved Road	⚐	Waterfall

ABOUT THE ELEVATION PROFILES

Each profile includes an elevation scale which approximately graphs the hills and dips on the route in height and distance. Please note that the scales on each profile are dramatically different. Scales may not always begin at an elevation of zero feet and height increments and distance can vary.

ABOUT THE RIDE PROFILES

Each profile includes a narrative description of the ride's setting and terrain. This description also includes mile-by-mile route directions, as well as information about the ride's highlights and unique attributes.

The rides marked by the **BEST** ◖ symbol are highlighted by the author.

Options

If alternative routes are available, this section is used to provide information on side trips or note how to shorten or lengthen the ride.

Driving Directions

This section provides detailed driving directions to the start of the route from the nearest major town.

Route Directions

Each profile includes a mile-by-mile listing of what to expect along the trail or road. Every major turn is noted and nearby sights or supplies are indicated where available.

ABOUT THE DIFFICULTY RATING

Each profile includes a difficulty rating. The ratings are defined as follows:

1: Beginners, families with young children, or anyone seeking a casual, recreational route will like these rides. They're mostly flat and usually less than 15 miles, or offer shorter options. Typically smooth-surfaced, they generally follow bike paths or rail trails with no vehicular traffic. Estimated ride times reflect the slower paces more appropriate for such trails, and more typical of beginner riders.

2: Novices with good fitness, families with older children, or anyone seeking a relatively casual recreational ride will like these rides. They avoid any difficult or technical features, and are generally less than 25 miles with little elevation gain. Off-road rides may involve varied surfaces, like gravel, ballast, or grass, but don't require technical mountain biking skills. Estimated ride times presume a similar pace to the previous category.

3: These rides are appropriate for cyclists with decent aerobic fitness and some cycling experience. Beginners may find them a little daunting. Road rides are generally less than 40 miles, but require moderate hill climbs, and may follow roads with broken pavement and some vehicle traffic. Off-road rides assume basic technical skills and comfort with rough and changing terrain—cyclists should have some experience on a variety of trails, including single-track. Estimated ride times reflect the faster pace of fitter riders.

4: Intermediate riders with excellent aerobic fitness will thrive on these routes, but anyone not used to longer rides with challenging features will be over-matched. Road rides are generally 30–60 miles, with steep climbs and descents, and may include sections with less-than-ideal surfaces or traffic conditions. Off-road rides presume solid technical skills and bike-handling, and involve steep climbs and descents over rough and changing conditions. Bikers should have solid experience on a variety of trails, including single-track. These rides may traverse less-traveled, more remote areas. Estimated ride times presume a faster pace.

5: These rides will challenge even fit riders. They should only be undertaken by experienced cyclists with excellent aerobic fitness. Road rides have several steep or prolonged hill climbs, and cover longer distances. Off-road rides are technical, on a variety of surfaces and types of trails, and require advanced bike handling skills. They will involve steep climbs and descents. Some riders may have to portage their bikes through sections. Estimated ride times presume a fast pace.

Biking Tips

Most people remember the thrill they felt the first time they rode a bike without training wheels. Part of what draws us to bikes is that each ride gives us the chance to feel that thrill again. Cycling is great exercise, efficient transportation, and a lot of fun—but it also involves risks and dangers. Observing the rules of the road or trail, following simple safety guidelines, and knowing the basics of how to repair and maintain your bike will ensure you many years of happy, trouble-free biking.

Want to get better at bicycling? Want to learn more about rides in your area, or find someone to ride with? Start with local bike shops. Most host group rides a couple days each week, with varied average speeds to attract different riders. Get online and see if there's a cycling club or advocacy group active in your area. Find a local race schedule and go watch, cheer, and mingle—most members of the cycling community like to talk about all things bike-related. Finally, get outside and ride, and say hello when you run into other riders.

BIKE SAFETY TIPS

The following tips can help make your ride safer, both for you and the people with whom you share the roads and trails.

Wear a Helmet

Above all else, helmets should fit properly. According to the Bicycle Helmet Safety Institute (www.bhsi.org), a good helmet should fit "level on your head, touching all around, comfortably snug but not tight. The helmet should not move more than about an inch in any direction, and must not pull off no matter how hard you try." You'll see a lot of riders wearing helmets incorrectly, pushed back off the forehead or with unbuckled straps. These are mistakes that can render the helmet ineffective. Helmets have a life span, and they should be inspected or replaced every few years and after every accident. If you're not sure how to choose a helmet or how to properly fit one, stop in at a bike shop and ask for help.

© CHRIS BERNARD

Rules of the Road

Bicycles and their place on the road is a controversial issue that seems to become more of a problem each year. Our road system was not designed for the shared use of motor vehicles and bicycles, nor was it designed even to handle the numbers of motor vehicles that travel it every day. Entire books have been written about bicycle safety and the rules of the road, but they can be summarized in a few simple rules.

- Bicycles belong on the road or in the bike lane, not on the sidewalk. When riding on a street or road, bicycles are vehicles—just like cars or trucks—and are subject to the same laws and regulations.
- Ride in the same direction as traffic.
- Stop at stop signs, traffic lights, and crosswalks.
- Signal your intention to turn.
- Use the appropriate lanes.
- Treat motorists with respect, because you're asking for theirs in return. In a car-meets-bike matchup, bikes don't stand a chance, so take your own safety seriously.
- Ride predictably. Don't swerve or dodge between cars, and whenever possible, make eye contact with drivers—don't ever assume they see you.
- Watch parked cars for opening doors.
- Use lights when riding at or after dusk.
- State bicycle laws vary, so be sure you're familiar with the laws in the state in which you are riding.

Rules of the Trail

Bicycles and their place on trails can be even more controversial. But a little common courtesy can go a long way.

- When riding off-road, on single- or double-track or fire roads, yield to other bikers and trail users, especially horses. Slow down and use caution when approaching or passing, and let others know you're coming.
- Stay on designated trails. Be aware of your environment—riding trails is a privilege, not a right, and as such is in constant jeopardy of being revoked.
- Don't use overly muddy trails where erosion is a concern, don't build unauthorized trail features or stunts, and stay on marked trails rather than short-cutting or making new trails.
- Don't harass wildlife or domestic animals, and be respectful of private property.

ON THE TRAIL

Riding a bike on rail trails and multiuse paths requires a distinct etiquette built

© CHRIS BERNARD

Keep to the right except when passing.

around common courtesy. Be prepared to share with other trail users: pedestrians, dog walkers, equestrians, in-line skaters, strollers, and other bikers.

Unless separate bike and pedestrian lanes are marked, keep to the right except when passing. Always ride in the direction of traffic, not against it; don't be a bike salmon. Keep your speed to what is safe for the conditions; heavily trafficked paths are not the place to practice your time trial skills. When overtaking another cyclist or pedestrian, call out to him or her well in advance to prevent spooking him or her—startled people have a tendency to veer in front of you. If you don't have a bell, say "On your left" loudly and firmly enough for the person to hear you. Watch for headphones, a sign that he or she hasn't heard you and has no idea you're approaching. Don't wear headphones yourself. If you *do* wear headphones, turn your music low enough to hear what's going on around you.

All cyclists will be judged by your actions, so act responsibly. If you see someone with bike problems, slow down or stop and ask if you can help. Do they need a spare tube or help changing a tire? Do they need a cell phone?

It's also worth noting that many other users will not be as considerate as you'd like them to be. Dog walkers will let their dogs wander to the far side of the path, turning leashes into guillotines; baby strollers will appear suddenly in front of you as the people pushing them make unannounced U-turns; pedestrians and joggers will swerve, veer, or stop without warning or concern for anyone behind them; other cyclists will speed by at leg-busting speeds, talking on cell phones; and in-line skaters will sway side-to-side, hogging the entire path.

Be patient, stay calm, ride defensively, and set a good example. Don't litter. And don't be a jerk. It's that simple.

Be Prepared

Plan your route and make sure you have a good map. Check the weather and dress for the day, and bring extra clothing or rain gear if necessary. Start early enough so you'll have plenty of daylight. If you are riding in a remote area, especially off-road, you'll need a little more preparation. Maps become essential, and you may need a road map as well as a topographic map, a compass, or a GPS device. If you're riding alone, tell someone your trip plans and consider taking a cell phone.

Know Your Bike

The more you get to know your bike, the more fun you'll have with it. Ensure you can make emergency roadside repairs and perform basic maintenance. If you don't know how or have trouble teaching yourself, take a bike repair or maintenance class. Perform a quick safety check before each ride: Check your wheels' quick-release skewers to make sure they're on right and tightly. Check your tire pressure. (Recommended tire pressures are marked on the tires' sidewalls. For mountain biking you'll typically want less pressure in the tires to get more contact with the ground.) Oil your chain. Check your brakes.

Basic Riding Techniques

Several techniques and tricks will help you improve and make it possible for you to ride safely on a wide range of surfaces. Learn to shift properly if your bike has multiple gears. If you don't know how to shift, learn from others, practice in an empty parking lot, or take a class.

Use your brakes wisely: Most of your braking power comes from the front brakes, but use them judiciously to avoid an "endo" (flipping up on your front wheel) or a "superman" (flipping over your handlebars). Learn to use a combination of front and back brakes. Don't squeeze too hard, or you'll lock up the wheels into a skid. Learn to brake before a curve or corner so you can ride through it at the right speed.

For mountain biking, move your weight back to lift the front wheel slightly to get over rocks and roots. On steep downhills, shift your weight back by sliding well back on the seat, or even off the seat and over the rear wheel if possible.

REPAIRS AND MAINTENANCE

Learning the basics of maintenance and upkeep will do more than keep your bike rolling safely and indefinitely; it will enhance your enjoyment. Nothing ruins a ride faster than equipment failure that could have been prevented—except maybe a bike suffering from a multitude of annoying malfunctions that persist throughout the entire ride.

Basic Maintenance

Basic maintenance you can perform on your bike includes learning to change flat tires, regularly checking the tightness of all bolts and connections, and above all, cleaning your bike regularly. As you clean it, inspect it for problems like frayed or rusty cables and nicked tires.

CLEANING

To wash your bike, use a repair stand, tree, or car-mounted bike rack, or hang it over a mailbox. Don't turn the bike upside down; water may get into bearings that need to stay dry. Rinse the bike first, either with a bucket of water or a garden hose on a gentle setting. Then get a bucket of warm, soapy water (dish soap is fine) and use it to scrub the bike gently with a brush or sponge. Don't forget to scrub the wheel rims, either now or with a rag when the bike is dry. Use a separate sponge for the chain and drivetrain. Rinse the bike off, then dry it with a chamois or soft towel. Then clean and lube the chain.

CHAINS

If there's only one thing you ever do to maintain your bike, that's it: clean the chain. This will make riding and shifting smoother and more efficient. It also keeps the chain from wearing down gears and eliminates the dead giveaway of an inexperienced cyclist—a squeaky chain. Wipe the chain off with a clean rag to get at the first layer of grease and grime. Then scrub all parts of the drive train, including the chain, crankset, derailleurs, and cassette (rear cogwheels). Use a citrus degreaser or other biodegradable solvent, and use a rag, small brush (such as an old toothbrush), screwdriver, or whatever tools seem to work. Rinse off the degreaser, and then shake the bike to dry it. When you're done, apply a small amount of lubricant to the chain and wipe off the excess.

Don't overlube the chain. It will only attract dirt and grit. And don't use WD-40—it's not a lubricant, it's a solvent. There are several types of chain lube to choose from, so ask at the bike shop and be sure to mention what type of riding you do.

SHIFTING

Adjusting your bike's shifting is not difficult, and it falls somewhere between art and science. Poor shifting is often the result of cables lacking sufficient tension to shift and hold the proper gears. Most bikes have barrel adjusters, or little knurled knobs, where the cable housings meet the shifters or the derailleurs—turn these adjusters one-quarter turn at a time to shorten the cable, and check the shifting after each turn. If you can't resolve the issue, it may be time for a new cable or an adjustment of the derailleur itself, a fix best made by an experienced mechanic.

BRAKING

Good braking relies on mechanical advantage between the brake lever and the amount of cable it can pull, forcing the brake pads against the wheel's rim. If your brakes don't provide enough stopping power, no matter how hard you squeeze them, you can try shortening the cable using the same method described for adjusting shifting—most brakes have barrel adjusters. You can also dry off your brake pads and see if that helps. If not, it may be time to replace the pads or cables or to have a professional mechanic adjust your brakes. This is not an area in which you can afford to mess up.

Roadside Repairs

The more you ride, the more you'll want to learn to fix your bike, because the more time you spend on it the better the odds that something will go wrong. Every cyclist, beginner or advanced, on- or off-road, needs to know how to fix a flat tire. Mountain bikers in particular should know how to fix a broken chain. From there, you can graduate to replacing broken cables or broken spokes, fixing bent rims, and so on. Many other repairs, adjustments, and fine-tuning can wait until you get home or take it to a bike shop.

FIXING A FLAT

Don't ride with a flat tire, don't rely on others to know how to fix one for you, and don't rely on a cell phone to get you out of a jam. Fixing a flat is quick and easy if you practice a few times. Get a bike repair manual, take a class, or have an experienced cyclist show you how to do it.

The basic steps: 1) Release the brake and remove the wheel. 2) Remove the valve cap, deflate the tire, and use tire levers to unseat the tire and remove the tube. 3) Inspect the tire, tube, and rim to find and remove the cause of the flat. 4) Replace the tube with a new one or patch the old one. 5) Put the tube and tire back on the wheel. 6) Inflate and seat the tire.

REPAIRING A BROKEN CHAIN

This requires a little more skill and knowledge about what type of chain you have on your bike. You'll also need a chain tool. (These are fairly small, inexpensive, and very useful.) If you are serious about cleaning your chain, you'll want one anyway, since the most thorough chain cleaning requires removing the chain from the derailleur. For a trailside repair, use the chain tool to push out the damaged pin or link. Use a replacement pin or link, and then use the chain tool to reconnect the chain. In an emergency, reconnect the chain at the next link, though a shorter chain will mean you will probably not have full use of your gears, so ride home cautiously.

BIKING GEAR CHECKLIST

You can fit the essentials into a small seat bag. If traveling by car to a trailhead, bring additional tools and supplies to leave in your vehicle. Know how to use everything on this list.

If you see another bicyclist stopped, ask if he or she needs help. Maybe someone will do the same for you, but don't count on it: be prepared to self-rescue.

Essential
- Allen wrench set (most bikes use metric bolts, but check yours)
- Cash and ID
- Chain tool (more important if you are mountain biking)
- Food (for longer rides)
- Lights (if riding after dark)
- Map
- Patch kit (replace when needed, as old glue can dry out)
- Premoistened hand wipes (if you need to put a slipped chain back on, you'll be glad you brought them)
- Pump or CO2 cartridge and injector
- Spare tube
- Tire levers

Recommended
- Biking gloves (padded gloves absorb road vibrations and protect your palms in the event of a fall)
- Biking shorts (same as the gloves, but for a different part of your body)
- Cell phone (as long as you don't rely on it to get you out of a tight spot)
- Compass (especially useful for off-road riding)
- Insect repellent (more important for off-road rides in the woods)
- Spare clothing
- Sunglasses or eye protection (essential if you wear contact lenses; nothing's worse than dirt, grit, or a piece of glass in your eye)

Additional
- Bike lock (you never know when you might want or need to leave your bike somewhere)
- Dry clothes (to change into)
- Duct tape (it holds the universe together)
- Extra water and food
- First-aid kit
- Oil and chain lubricant
- Rags or towels (if it's raining or muddy, you'll want to wipe off your frame and tires)
- Sunscreen and lip balm
- Tools (wrenches, a multitool with screwdrivers and a blade, spoke wrench)

MASSACHUSETTS

© GEORGE BURBA / 123RF.COM

BEST BIKE RIDES

During mountain biking's nascent years, the dirt trails, fire roads, and single-track of Massachusetts's state forests started seeing an influx of fat-tire traffic. These roots-and-rocks trails spawned a lot of recreational cyclists and more than a few pros, including Jesse Anthony and national cyclocross champ Tim Johnson, both of whom grew up in the northeastern part of the state.

As the trails' popularity increased, so did their number, thanks in large part to the New England Mountain Biking Association (NEMBA). The recreational trails advocacy organization is a membership-based group with nearly 20 chapters in New England. Collectively, the group advocates for recreational use, gives grants for trail projects, provides volunteers for trail maintenance and protection, and organizes bicycle patrols. In 2003 NEMBA became the first bike advocacy group in the country to buy, own, and manage property with its purchase of a 47-acre trail network in Milford. Known informally as "Vietnam," these trails draw mountain bikers from all over the region. Mixing a variety of terrains with hardcore natural obstacles and laced with purpose-built stunts and features, they've become the standard by which other trails are judged.

In Massachusetts, Vietnam's no anomaly. You'll find outstanding off-road trails all over the state. Sharpen your skills on the rugged Grizzly Adams and Old Florida Road rides in the mountainous northwest, where you're likely to have miles of single-track and dirt roads to yourself. Tackle the Trail of Tears on Cape Cod, a remarkably wild patch of woods just minutes from both beach and highway. Bomb through the fast corners of the Beaver Pond trail in central Massachusetts or the fire roads and root-strewn single-track of the Harold Parker and Willowdale state forests in the northeast.

If white-knuckle woodland rides aren't your cup of tea, don't worry – the state's roads, rail trails, and bike paths offer a menu of rides to sate the hunger of pedalers of all abilities. Push your legs and lungs to their limits on the ferocious climbs of Wachusett Mountain, a little more than an hour from Boston, or Mount Greylock, which looms over tourist-friendly Williamstown. Tour the scenic coastal stretches between historic Salem and gorgeous Cape Ann, pedaling past famous landmarks and photo opportunities. Try to tear your friends' legs off on the long, fast loops around Quabbin Reservoir, or just spend a relaxing day rolling with the family on the Nashua River or Cape Cod rail trails.

There are many routes not covered here, including the Minuteman Bikeway, an incredibly popular commuter path through Bedford, Lexington, Arlington, and Cambridge, or the new Bruce Freeman Rail Trail in Chelmsford, a promising route still under construction at the time of publication. With so many to choose from, deciding which routes to include proved challenging, and you may find it equally daunting deciding which to ride.

Lest you think Massachusetts an unmitigated cyclists' paradise, a simple caveat: Traffic can be unreasonable, especially in the eastern part of the state, and especially during summer in the many touristy areas.

The good news is that with so many routes available, you can time them so you're on a vehicle-free rail trail or deep in the woods when everyone else is angrily bumper-to-bumper on the roads. You'll be pedaling contentedly into a Berkshire Mountains sunset when the roads are empty.

1 WANDERING WILLIAMSTOWN
Williamstown

PAVED ROADS WITH MODERATE TRAFFIC

Difficulty: 3	**Total Distance:** 29.1 miles
Riding Time: 2.5 hours	**Elevation Gain:** 1,495 feet

Summary: This hilly ride runs through an artsy college town; it's high on scenery, but also on traffic.

Williamstown is, in many ways, the quintessential college town. The ride starts there, and you're likely to see local cyclists along this popular route. More than most in this book, this ride relies on roads well-traveled by vehicles. While the pavement is generally good and the shoulders wide, if you're not comfortable sharing the road with traffic, skip this one.

That said, the traffic is not bad—Williamstown is not exactly downtown Boston in terms of urban density or population—and the rewards are worth the annoyances on this hilly loop through one of many scenic corners of the Berkshires. Among the payoffs are the stunning views of Massachusetts's highest peak, Mount Greylock.

Leaving Williamstown on MA-43, you'll crisscross the Green River as neighborhoods turn from residential to pastoral. Where MA-43 and US-7 meet, you'll

© CHRIS BERNARD

Mapped out in the shadow of Mount Greylock, this ride explores the popular downtown area of Williamstown and surrounding towns.

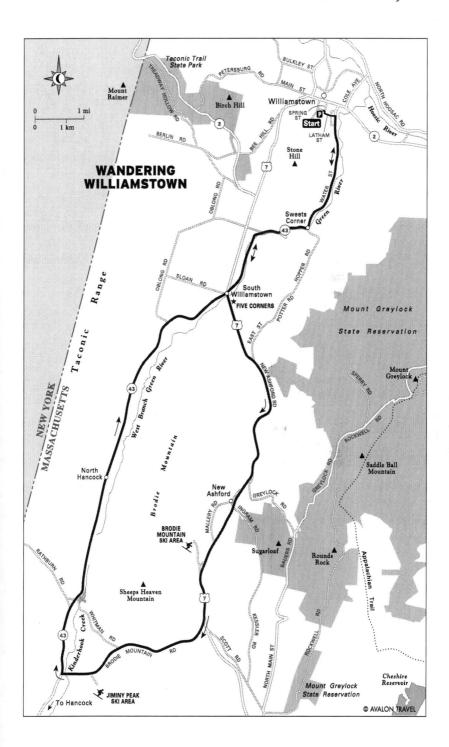

WANDERING
WILLIAMSTOWN

find the historic Store at Five Corners, which dates to 1762, with a café, supplies, restrooms, ice cream, homemade fudge, picnic tables, and more.

You'll then climb US-7, a fast and busy road with a wide, smooth shoulder, making a gradual ascent between two mountain ranges, one smooth and rolling (to the west) and one punctuated with sharp peaks and the 3,491-foot-high summit of Greylock (to the east).

Leave the traffic behind. In its place, face a long, steep climb up the winding Brodie Mountain Road, followed by a long, screaming downhill to the base of ski resort Jiminy Peak.

The return ride on MA-43 starts with a climb, then turns to a gentle rolling up-and-down ride through farmlands and fields with great mountain views and a gentle coast back to where you began.

For more information, contact the Williamstown Chamber of Commerce, P.O. Box 357, Williamstown, MA 01267, 413/458-9077 or 800/214-3799, www .williamstownchamber.com.

Options

Feel like a challenge? A big one? Add the summit of Mount Greylock, with a 2,785-foot ascent and an additional 20 miles or so, to this ride by turning left at Mile 12 onto US-7/New Ashford Road, and bearing left onto Scott Road. At Mile 2.3 of the option, turn left onto Greylock Road, and begin climbing. At Mile 2.75, turn left onto Rockwell Road and enter Mount Greylock State Reservation. Turn right at Mile 10.5 onto the road to the summit, which you'll reach in 0.8 mile. Soak in the views, put on some armwarmers for the descent, and turn around. To return, turn right onto Notch Road for a fast, winding descent. Turn left and then right to stay on Notch Road, eventually turning left to return to MA-2.

Locals' Tip: The Indian food at Spice Root (23 Spring Street, Williamstown, MA 01267, 413/458-5200) is a pleasant surprise and a good, flavorful way to cap a day of riding.

Places to Stay: The (relatively) affordable Maple Terrace Inn (555 Main Street, Williamstown, MA 01267, 413/458-9677, http://mapleterrace.com) is right downtown, near the art museums, and the owners are friendly.

Driving Directions

From points south, take US-7 to Williamstown. From points east, take MA-2 to Williamstown. From MA-2 (Main Street), turn south onto the one-way Spring Street, a busy shopping street. Drive 0.2 mile to the end of Spring Street, where you'll find several public parking lots. Williamstown has plenty of supplies, lodging options, and bike shops.

Route Directions

0.0 From the Spring Street parking lot, turn RIGHT onto Spring Street and bear LEFT onto Latham Street.

0.3 Turn RIGHT onto Water Street (MA-43).

5.0 Turn LEFT onto US-7. *Supplies available at the Store at Five Corners.*

12.0 Turn RIGHT onto Brodie Mountain Road. OPTION: Turn left onto US-7/New Ashford Road and follow option directions.

14.8 *Supplies available at Jiminy Peak ski resort.*

15.4 Turn RIGHT onto MA-43.

24.0 Go STRAIGHT across US-7, staying on MA-43, which becomes Water Street.

28.8 Turn LEFT onto Latham Road.

29.1 Turn RIGHT onto Spring Street and immediate LEFT to return to parking lot.

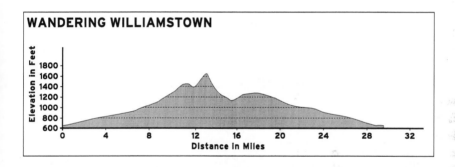

WANDERING WILLIAMSTOWN

2 GRIZZLY ADAMS

Mount Greylock State Reservation, New Ashford

SINGLE-TRACK, DOUBLE-TRACK, DIRT ROADS

Difficulty: 4   **Total Distance:** 8.5 miles

Riding Time: 1.5 hours   **Elevation Gain:** 1,200 feet

Summary: This challenging, climbing mountain route offers rough, remote conditions – definitely not for beginners.

If you're a mountain biker visiting the Mount Greylock area, you're going to want to sample the trails that snake around the mountainside. This ride is a good example of what's there. Almost all double-track, it's not particularly technical, but there's a good, fast descent followed by an equally good climb that will leave most riders fighting for breath—and traction.

The first part of the trail is smooth. It covers wide, grassy trails and loose dirt on what could be considered a road, if it were anywhere a vehicle could access it. But just a mile or so into it, the ride begins dropping obstacles in your path—ruts, tree stumps, rocks, downed branches—that will make any mountain biker worth his or her salt happy.

Then it becomes more difficult. The trail narrows and steepens—first downhill, then up—and obstacles increase in frequency. Decomposing grass and leaves can be slick and hide stumps, roots, and rocks. Pricker bushes seem to reach out

© CHRIS BERNARD

Riders who put in the effort are in for a treat on the Old Adams Road mountain bike trail, beginning high atop Mount Greylock.

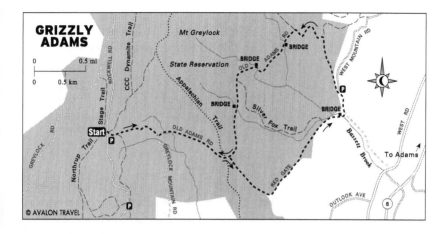

for your legs and wheels. Noises in the woods around you seem louder, closer, and spookier than they should. Bring a spare tube and air pump; you don't want to be stuck here.

A series of climbs begin around the time you hear a noisy mountain stream, which will distract you from the sound of your own panting and gasping. The real challenge is maintaining your momentum—small stones, branches, and roots will fight your traction, and once you're stopped, starting again is very difficult. Near the end of the trail, you'll pass through an area rife with wild raspberry bushes that, in season, are worth stopping for. (After the climb, you'll be grateful for any excuse to stop.)

Note that the road to the parking area is open from late May through November 1, weather permitting. For more information, contact Mount Greylock State Reservation Visitors Center, 30 Rockwell Road, P.O. Box 138, Lanesborough, MA 01237, 413/499-4262, www.mass.gov/dcr/parks/mtGreylock/.

Options

To expand this ride with some serious climbing, park at the base of Goodell Road where it meets US-7, just north of New Ashford, and ride up Goodell Road/Greylock Road to Rockwell Road, taking a right on paved Rockwell Road and riding less than 1 mile to the parking area where this route begins. Goodell Road is a loose dirt road that snakes precipitously up the side of Mount Greylock. Though it's less than 4 miles long, it climbs 1,227 feet over that distance. Riding to and from the route below would add nearly 10 miles of riding—and a lot of climbing. Be careful on the descent.

This ride is near Wandering Williamstown, Ashuwillticook Rail Trail, and Old Florida Road.

Locals' Tip: Grab a bite and a beverage and enjoy a view of Pontoosuc Lake at Matt Reilly's Restaurant (750 South Main Street, Lanesborough, MA 01237, 413/447-9780) just south of Mount Greylock.

Places to Stay: The Lanesborough Country Inn (499 South Main Street, Lanesborough, MA 01237, 413/442-1009, www.lanesboroughcountryinn.com) is a reasonably priced accommodation, with 10 custom-built log cabins in addition to rooms.

Driving Directions

From US-7 North, turn right on North Main Street in Lanesborough, and almost a mile later, right again on Quarry Road, watching for signs for the visitors center. Turn left onto Rockwell Road. The visitors center is half a mile up on your right and has facilities and maps. The parking area for the trail, known as the "Jones Nose" lot, is another 4 miles up Rockwell Road on your right.

Route Directions

0.0 From the far end of the parking area, beside the signs, follow the Old Adams Road Mountain Bicycle Trail, grassy double-track winding around a gate.

0.4 Turn LEFT, and then LEFT again, following signs for Old Adams Road. The trail turns to dirt.

1.5 Stay STRAIGHT at the intersection with the Appalachian Trail. Watch for hikers.

1.6 At the intersection, turn RIGHT onto double-track. This snowmobile trail is called Red Gate Trail.

2.2 Stay STRAIGHT over rough bridge. Crossing the bridge can be sketchy, so be careful.

2.4 At bottom of short descent, stay STRAIGHT past logging road.

2.5 Turn RIGHT onto logging road.

2.6 Enter a clearing, and begin descent. Stay straight past next few trail entrances.

3.2 Turn LEFT (downhill).

3.3 Turn LEFT over a bridge, then RIGHT over second bridge.

3.5 Turn LEFT, sharply, onto West Mountain Road double-track.

4.0 A rocky uphill leads to a large, dirty parking area. Cross the lot into the field and follow the signs to the LEFT for Cheshire Harbor Bicycle Trail.

4.1 Behind a gate, the real climb begins.

4.8 Switchbacks signal that you're nearing the top of the climb.

5.1 Turn LEFT onto Old Adams Road, and cross a bridge.

6.1 Begin another uphill section, this one laced with rocks and other obstacles.

7.8 Turn RIGHT (uphill).

8.5 END at parking area.

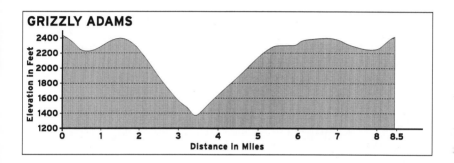

3 ASHUWILLTICOOK RAIL TRAIL   BEST **C**
Lanesborough, Cheshire, and Adams

WIDE, PAVED RAIL TRAIL

Difficulty: 2   **Total Distance:** 22 miles

Riding Time: 3 hours   **Elevation Gain:** 62 feet

Summary: A wide, flat rail trail through the heart of the Berkshires, this ride is suitable for cyclists of all skill levels.

The 10-foot-wide Ashuwillticook Rail Trail is paved its entire length, paralleling MA-8 and offering cyclists and pedestrians a safe and scenic way to commute, recreate, or just to commune with nature. This is everything a rail trail should be.

The rail corridor began in 1845 when the Pittsfield and North Adams Railroad wanted to connect Rutland, Vermont, with the Housatonic Railroad in the south. Over the years, ownership of the track changed as the rail lines were acquired or merged, until the Boston & Maine bought it in 1981. Rail services were abandoned in 1990.

Since then, the trail has seen a lot of use, and on any given day, you're likely to meet cyclists, runners, walkers, and in-line skaters. In the winter, add snowshoers and cross-country skiers. Ride down the trail on a sunny day in early September,

© CHRIS BERNARD

Paved, smooth, and wide throughout its entire length, the Ashuwillticook Rail Trail is an excellent place for riders of all ages and abilities.

and it's easy to understand its popularity. The paved surface is smooth and flat, the views are spectacular, and the foliage—even this early in the season—adds eye-catching color.

Whether you're on the trail's more rural first third, along the water's edge that hems the Cheshire Reservoir, or the on the final here-and-there sections crossing through downtown, the Ashuwillticook is a perfectly pleasant ride—in fact, the name means "the pleasant river in between the hills."

For more information, contact the Massachusetts Department of Conservation and Recreation in Adams, Massachusetts, 413/442-8928, www.mass.gov/dcr/parks/western/asrt.htm.

Options

This trail is rideable by just about anyone, including beginners and small children. Mileage is marked on the pavement, so you can decide exactly how far you want to go before you turn around. Alternatively, leave a car at the far end, in Cheshire (halfway), or just beyond there at Farnam's Causeway on Cheshire Reservoir. Parking is free and available at either end.

This ride is near Wandering Williamstown, Grizzly Adams, and Old Florida Road.

Locals' Tip: The Miss Adams Diner (53 Park Street, Adams, MA 01220, 413/743-5300) is a retro-looking diner that will meet all the expectations of diner lovers and satiate appetites earned after a long, lazy ride on the rail trail.

Places to Stay: The Topia Inn (10 Pleasant Street, Adams, MA 01220, 413/743-9605, http://topiainn.com) is a environmentally friendly inn powered entirely by solar panels and biodiesel. It's a high-end experience for self-indulgence.

Driving Directions

From points north, east, or west, take MA-2 in downtown North Adams to MA-8 south for 5.5 miles to Adams center. (Look for brown Ashuwillticook signs.) Turn left onto Hoosac Street, then immediately right onto Depot Street. Parking is on the left at Discover the Berkshires Visitors Center (3 Hoosac Street, www .berkshires.org, daily 8:30 A.M.–5 P.M.). Access to the rail trail is behind the Visitors Center.

From points south, take I-90 (the Mass Pike) to exit 2 in Lee and follow US-20 west to US-7 North for 11 miles to downtown Pittsfield. At Park Square rotary, follow East Street for 3.25 miles (East Street becomes Merrill Road after 1.5 miles) to the intersection of MA-9 and MA-8. Continue straight through the intersection on MA-8 north for 1.5 miles to the Lanesborough-Pittsfield line. Turn left at lights for the Berkshire Mall Road entrance and rail trail parking.

Route Directions

0.0 From Adams, head south on the rail trail.

2.1 This is one of the quieter sections of the trail.

5.5 Cheshire Reservoir is on your right. (It can be windy here.)

6.9 Cross Farnam's Causeway, which offers trail access and parking. *Restrooms available off the trail to the right. Park benches offer a nice lunch spot with beautiful views of the reservoir.*

11.0 End of rail trail at Berkshire Mall in Lanesborough. *Restrooms available.* TURN AROUND.

15.0 Cross Farnam's Causeway.

22.0 END at parking area.

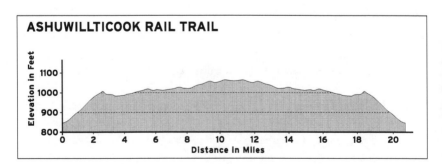

4 OLD FLORIDA ROAD
Savoy Mountain State Forest

SINGLE-TRACK, DOUBLE-TRACK, DIRT ROADS

Difficulty: 5   **Total Distance:** 7 miles

Riding Time: 2 hours   **Elevation Gain:** 763 feet

Summary: This rugged, backwoods trail will test your endurance, fitness level, and tolerance.

Buggy. Wet. Remote. Poorly marked. Rocky. Muddy. Buggy. Each of those words describes this ride, and that's right, "buggy" gets listed twice. But for those of you who like bushwhacking rides that challenge your sense of adventure as well as your legs and lungs, this is one.

A world apart from some of the state forest rides in the eastern part of the state, this route through Savoy Mountain State Forest—carved out of the Hoosac Range, an extension of the Green Mountains—will have you panting before you even start pedaling. The vertiginous drive along MA-2 to reach the entrance road gives you an idea of the remoteness of the area.

Some of the forest was originally cleared and used as farmland, and there are

© ADAM CLOUGH

Deep in the woods and away from civilization, Old Florida Road can be muddy — and the bugs can be fierce.

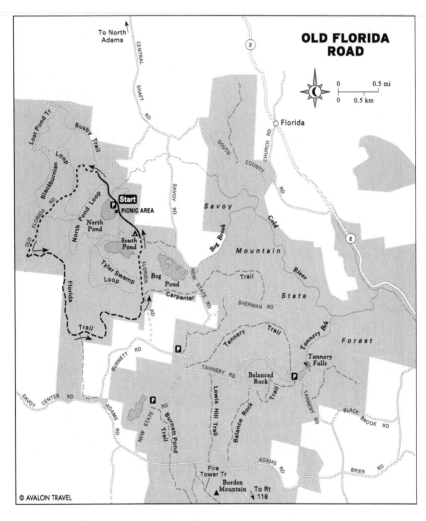

OLD FLORIDA ROAD

a few concrete dams, as well as some stands of apple trees and secondary forests of Norway and blue spruce mixed in with older hardwoods. You'll find a picnic area, a campground, cabins, two ponds for swimming and fishing, full facilities, and lots of trails to explore.

This route takes you along Old Florida Road counterclockwise from North Pond. From the main entrance road, you pass through Tower Swamp—hence the bugs—before climbing a very rocky trail. After a tough series of downs and ups, the trail heads east. Though most of the trail is technical and rocky, a few late stretches in a pine forest are fun and fast. If you have a GPS unit or a compass, bring it. This is a remote trail that's not well-marked, and it's easy to get lost.

In spring, in early summer, and during exceptionally rainy periods, you're likely to encounter mudpits too deep to ride through. While you're carrying your bike through them, knee deep in the muck, the bugs will feast on you. These trails are designed for all-terrain vehicles, and it shows. You'll also pass several hiking trails. Please don't ride them—they're off-limits to bikes and doing so ruins it for everyone else.

The park is open from 8 A.M. until dusk year-round. For more information, contact Savoy Mountain State Forest, Central Shaft Road, Savoy, MA 413/663-8469, www.state.ma.us/dem/parks/svym.htm.

Options

For a slightly less strenuous ride, follow Florida Road south to a large dirt parking lot, where you pick up the unpaved, rough Tannery Road past Balanced Rock and Tannery Falls, a dramatic plunging waterfall. It's not a bad ride to reach the rock, but it's hilly to Tannery Falls, and you have to leave your bike and hike in a short distance to see them.

Locals' Tip: There's not much food to be had around the park, so packing a lunch is a good bet.

Places to Stay: The campground is open mid-May to mid-October. For reservations, visit www.reserveamerica.com and search for Savoy Mountain State Forest. Some cabins are available.

Driving Directions

From North Adams and points west, take MA-2 east to the small town of Florida. Turn left onto Church Road and follow it to S. County Road. Turn right onto S. County Road and drive to Central Shaft Road, turning left. Drive 3.7 miles to the park's North Pond parking area, just past the boat launch. The parking fee is $5. North Pond has fishing, swimming, and full facilities with water and restrooms. Supplies and a bike shop are available in North Adams.

Route Directions

0.0 From North Pond parking lot, go LEFT on Central Shaft Road (toward park exit).

0.5 Turn LEFT onto Old Florida Road.

0.6 Turn RIGHT at fork.

0.8 Cross a stream on rock slabs.

2.9 Bear LEFT, following snowmobile signs, into a rocky clearing.
Trail continues to the right of the clearing, then takes an immediate
LEFT.

4.1 Turn LEFT, following the main trail.

5.6 Cross a clearing to a row of boulders, and turn LEFT onto unmarked
dirt road. OPTION: To check out Balanced Rock and Tannery
Falls, turn RIGHT instead of left onto the unmarked Florida Road.
Head south for about 1 mile to a large dirt parking lot and pick
up the unpaved, rough Tannery Road that leads to these natural
features.

7.0 END at North Pond parking area.

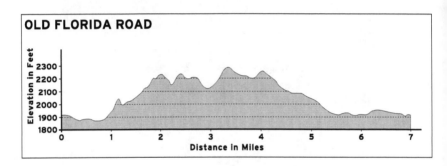

5 BARDWELLS FERRY LOOP
Shelburne Falls

PAVED ROADS WITH MINIMAL TO MODERATE TRAFFIC, DIRT ROAD

Difficulty: 4 **Total Distance:** 27.5 miles

Riding Time: 3 hours **Elevation Gain:** 2,440 feet

Summary: A relatively short – and relatively hilly – climbers' route, this loop highlights the rural backcountry of the river valley.

Shelburne Falls is a fun little place with a thriving downtown, which will catch you off-guard if you've visited some of the other little towns and villages in the region. Artistic and friendly, it's home to galleries, shops, studios, museums, and a handful of restaurants and cafés. And it's actually two towns, blending with the town of Buckland on the other side of the Deerfield River.

Two bridges span the river—the Iron Bridge and the pedestrian-only Bridge of Flowers, said to be the only one of its kind. A former trolley bridge, the concrete span is now completely overcome by gardens and flowers that bloom continuously thanks to volunteer efforts. Before or after your ride, stroll across this landmark, the connecting centerpiece of the towns.

This route gets you into the hills of the Berkshires on some beautiful backcountry roads with few cars or houses. There's a long climb out of Shelburne Falls and

From Shelburne Falls, or neighboring Buckland, the pedestrian-only Bridge of Flowers is worth a stop.

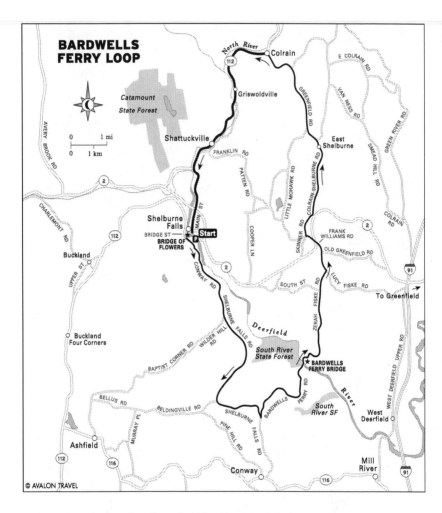

a steep downhill with a sharp backhand turn at the bottom to Bardwells Ferry Road. A few steep hills and some uneven pavement take you from woodlands into more open farmlands, and as you crest the last hill you get outstanding rural views of the river valley. Zip down toward the river and cross high above the water under the red spans of the 1882 Bardwells Ferry Bridge, a Massachusetts Historic Civil Engineering Landmark.

You'll pass farm stands and farmlands, woods and fields, and spend a good amount of time climbing. Savor the view, and savor the downhill that brings you into the village of Colrain.

The route follows the North River all the way back, with a mountain looming on your left and heavy industry (hydropower plants and factories) along the river on your right. You'll cross the river twice before going underneath MA-2 and riding back into Shelburne Falls.

The village information center has maps and restrooms. Make sure you walk across the Bridge of Flowers and look at the glacial potholes (access from Deerfield Avenue), carved out by the river. For more information, contact the Shelburne Falls Area Business Association and Village Information Center, 75 Bridge Street, Shelburne Falls, MA 01370, 413/625-2544, www.shelburnefalls.com.

Options

To extend this ride, from the finish head right on MA-112, following it counterclockwise as it winds its way south to Ashfield. Turn left on MA-116 in Ashfield, left on Baptist Corner Road, and left on Conway Road back to the starting point. This loop adds 18 miles and another 900 feet of climbing to the ride.

Locals' Tip: Christopher's Grinders (55 State Street, Shelburne Falls, MA 01370, 413/625-2345, www.christophersgrinders.com), just north of town on MA-112, is a great place (with a great name) to grab a sandwich or a slice of pizza.

Places to Stay: The Dancing Bear Guest House (22 Mechanic Street, Shelburne Falls, MA 01370, 413/625-9281, www.dancingbearguesthouse.com) is a small, charming bed-and-breakfast in a historic home right downtown.

Driving Directions

From points north and south, take MA-91 to Greenfield and take MA-2 west (exit 26). Drive 9 miles and take MA-2A (at the Sweetheart Restaurant) to Shelburne Falls. MA-2A becomes Bridge Street. Drive 0.3 mile and turn right onto Main Street. There's a public parking lot on the left, where this route begins. Supplies are available in Shelburne Falls. The closest bike shops are in Greenfield.

Route Directions

0.0 From the public parking lot, turn RIGHT onto Main Street.

0.1 Turn RIGHT onto Bridge Street; go across the Iron Bridge.

0.3 Turn LEFT along the river onto Conway Road (this becomes Shelburne Falls Road).

7.5 Make a sharp LEFT onto Bardwells Ferry Road.

10.4 Cross Bardwells Ferry Bridge.

11.8 Turn RIGHT at fork onto Zerah Fiske Road.

13.1 Go STRAIGHT through intersection, continuing on Zerah Fiske Road.

14.1 Continue STRAIGHT at a four-way intersection onto a dirt road.

14.5 Cross MA-2 (use extreme care) to Frank Williams Road.

14.7 Turn RIGHT onto Skinner Road (unmarked).

15.5 Turn LEFT onto Colrain-Shelburne Road.

20.8 Turn LEFT onto MA-112. *Supplies available at general store in Colrain.*

21.8 *Supplies available at general store in Griswoldville.*

26.8 Go under MA-2. Continue on MA-112, which becomes Main Street. OPTION: Head RIGHT on MA-112 and follow option directions.

27.5 Turn RIGHT into public parking lot just before Bridge Street.

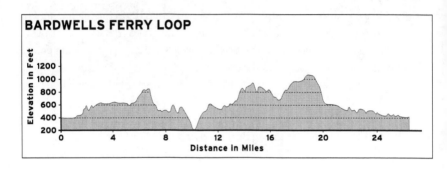

BARDWELLS FERRY LOOP

6 BEAVER POND LOOP
Otter River State Forest, Baldwinville

DIRT ROADS, DOUBLE-TRACK

Difficulty: 2   **Total Distance:** 8.7 miles

Riding Time: 1.5-2 hours   **Elevation Gain:** 156 feet

Summary: A network of fast trails in a surprisingly wild forest, this ride is suitable for most cyclists.

The Otter River State Forest seems like a more wild, remote place than it actually is. For a time, much of the forest was turned to farmland, but the Civilian Conservation Corps reseeded it—be thankful for their work as you meander through the shady woods. And riding the more than 100 miles of dirt roads and trails there, you'll find yourself forgetting you're just minutes from urban civilization. These trails offer riders of all abilities something to savor, and you can pick and choose the difficulty and length of any given ride.

This particular route is suitable for most riders, and begins on the wide, smooth, unpaved New Boston Road. (You can also camp here and begin your ride from the campground.) The first few turns lead deeper into the woods on bumpy roads, then double-track, and eventually nontechnical single-track.

The swampy areas and ponds make mosquitoes a real problem, so don't forget the bug repellent. The trails are not all marked, many small tempting single-track

© CHRIS BERNARD

The Beaver Pond trails are miles of phenomenal single-track in need of mountain bikers seeking a thrill.

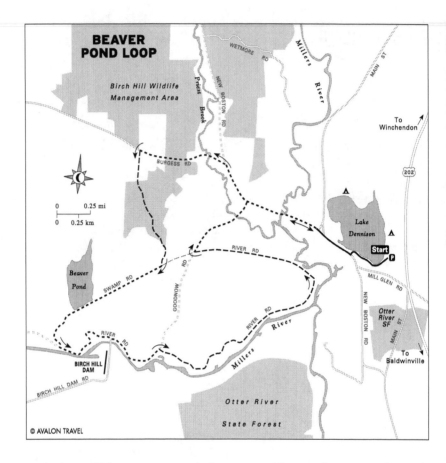

trails shoot off the main ones, and it's quite possible to get lost even with a trail map, available from the ranger station.

For the most part, this ride is suitable for a cyclocross bike. A mountain bike would be even better, but dual suspension is overkill.

The park hours are 10 A.M.–8 P.M. For more information, contact Otter River State Forest, New Winchendon Road, Baldwinville, MA 01436, 978/939-8962, www.state.ma.us/dem/parks/ottr.htm.

Options

To extend the ride, or to make it more challenging, around Mile 1.2 follow signs for the Wetmore Trail Loop. Or grab a trail map and explore on your own—there are plenty of options to choose from.

This ride is a reasonable driving distance from Reservoir Dogs and Wachusett Mountain.

Locals' Tip: Since the 1930s, locals have lined up at Lee's Hot Dog Stand (31 Central Street, Baldwinville, MA 01436, 978/939-5346) for foot-long dogs with all sorts of toppings, plus sides from clams to ice cream.

Places to Stay: The campground on site (New Winchendon Road, Baldwinville, MA 01436, 978/939-8962, www.state.ma.us/dem/parks/ottr.htm) offers 85 sites, flush toilets, showers, and out-your-tent-flap access to the trails.

Driving Directions

From points east or west, take MA-2 to exit 20 (Baldwinville Road). Drive 2.5 miles to a flashing red light. Turn right on Maple Street and pass through Baldwinville. Maple Street becomes MA-202. After 1.2 miles you'll see the main entrance to Otter River State Forest; pass this entrance and take the second entrance 1 mile farther down the road. Take the winding access road to Lake Dennison and park in the large parking lot on the right. The $5 day-use fee gets you access to a swimming beach at the lake, a campground, many picnic areas, and restrooms with flush toilets and water. Supplies are available in Baldwinville and the nearest bike shop is in Gardner.

Route Directions

0.0 START from the parking lot along the paved road with the lake on your right.

0.3 Turn LEFT onto wide dirt road.

0.9 Turn RIGHT onto New Boston Road at the intersection.

1.2 Turn LEFT onto Burgess Road. OPTION: Follow signs for the Wetmore Trail Loop.

1.8 Cross the town line into Baldwinville. The road becomes a paved road.

1.9 Turn LEFT onto trail. Follow orange blazes onto Swamp Road (unmarked).

2.2 Continue STRAIGHT on main trail at fork in path.

2.8 Turn RIGHT at intersection following blue trail markers.

3.3 Pass Beaver Pond on right.

3.8 Turn LEFT at the junction.

4.3 The trail comes to an L-shaped junction. Turn LEFT through the yellow gate into a field.

4.4 Follow trail along a chain-link fence; the dam is on the right.

4.7 Turn RIGHT at intersection on River Road (unmarked) through an orange gate. There is a yellow gate to the left.

6.8 Continue STRAIGHT at four-way intersection.

7.2 Turn RIGHT at junction with Goodnow Road (unmarked).

7.8 Turn RIGHT at intersection on New Boston Road.

8.4 Turn RIGHT onto paved road.

8.7 Return to parking lot.

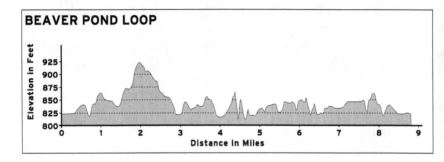

7 RESERVOIR DOGS

BEST **C**

Barre, Hardwick, and Petersham

PAVED, MOSTLY RURAL ROADS WITH SOME UNEVEN PAVEMENT AND MINIMAL TRAFFIC

Difficulty: 4

Total Distance: 45.7 miles

Riding Time: 3.5 hours

Elevation Gain: 3,260 feet

Summary: A hilly rural ride popular with road racers, this scenic route will also appeal to any cyclist who can handle the distance and climbs.

In the 1930s, the state flooded four towns in the Swift River valley to create one of the largest manufactured public water supplies in the country. Homes, businesses, and farms were moved, sold, or destroyed. Land was cleared and burned. The central Massachusetts landscape changed forever.

These days, the 18-mile-long Quabbin Reservoir is popular with anglers, but the area surrounding it draws cyclists. The land is hilly and beautiful and the roads untrafficked and rural—especially in the Ware River Reservation watershed area, protected and managed by the state's Metropolitan District Commission.

If you ride slowly, you'll notice the scenery and the wildlife. If you stop often, you can explore the small villages along the route and meet some of the people who give the area its personality. The area seems untouched by time and commercialism,

© J992875 | DREAMSTIME.COM

The ride around Quabbin Reservoir is a hilly treat for racers and confident riders who might feel a little less confident at the end of a long and tiring day.

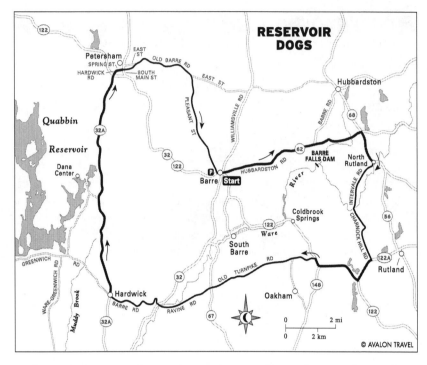

with town commons and general stores that provide just about anything either a cyclist or a community could need.

If you don't ride slowly, you're not alone. The area is training ground for a lot of New England road racers, and home to a race each year. You're likely to see packs of flat-backed, Lycra-clad warriors prowling this route.

The ride begins in Barre, where an expansive town common offers a gazebo and benches surrounded by diners, ice-cream shops, a bike store, and a visitors center. A steep descent takes you out of town into a rural, wooded area, past the entrance to Barre Falls Dam, an Army Corps of Engineers site. (If you're in no rush, ride the mile out and back for great vistas, a look at the impressive dam, and a recreation area with picnic tables and facilities.)

After a short stretch on the fast-moving MA-68, the ride heads onto smooth backcountry roads at the edge of the Ware River Reservation, lined with stone walls and historic markers and old cemeteries. The roads are also hilly—especially on Old Turnpike Road as you pass from woodlands into open pasturelands. The steepest climb comes on the way to Hardwick, but the scenery makes it worthwhile. Closer to town, the views change from farms and pastures to historic white houses with picket fences, impressive gardens, and well-kept stone walls. Hardwick's town common is a great meeting or stopping point, and the general store has restrooms, a deli counter, and a porch where cyclists tend to gather.

The next stretch, on MA-32A, follows the eastern edge of the Quabbin, with occasional views of the 181-mile shoreline, before visiting the town of Petersham. There's one more hilly stretch before finishing the final descent back into Barre.

For more information, contact the Central Quabbin Area Tourism Association, P.O. Box 95, Barre, MA 01005, www.centralquabbin.org.

Options

To extend your ride by 30 miles, in a circle around the reservoir, turn left at Mile 27 onto MA-32 and then bear right onto MA-9 West. After 15 miles, turn right onto MA-202 north. After 20 miles, turn right onto MA-122, rejoining the main route at Mile 45. The entire ride becomes 76 miles long.

Locals' Tip: The Upperdeck Sports Bar and Grille (377 Stetson Road, Barre, MA 01005, 978/355-2224) faces the slopes at Pine Ridge Snow Park.

Places to Stay: The Inn at Clamber Hill (111 North Main Street, Petersham, MA 01366, 978/724-8800, www.clamberhill.com) is a picturesque getaway on conservation land, a relaxing way to end a tiring day.

Driving Directions

From Worcester, take MA-122 west for approximately 20 miles to Barre. As you enter the center of town, bear right around the large town common onto Exchange Street. You'll find free parking lots around the common and a large lot on the eastern edge. Supplies and a bike shop are available in Barre.

Route Directions

0.0 From Exchange Street in the center of Barre, turn RIGHT onto Mechanic Street (this becomes Hubbardston Road/MA-62).

2.5 Continue STRAIGHT. *A right turn will take you on an optional side trip to Barre Falls Dam.*

6.8 Turn RIGHT onto MA-68.

8.2 Turn RIGHT onto Intervale Road.

10.6 Bear LEFT onto Charnock Hill Road.

13.1 Turn RIGHT onto MA-122A.

14.1 Turn RIGHT onto MA-122. *Small roadside picnic area.*

16.6 Turn LEFT onto Old Turnpike Road.

21.7 Continue STRAIGHT through intersection onto Ravine Road.

24.3 Continue STRAIGHT through intersection onto Barre Road.
Supplies available at Cloverhill Country Store farm stand.

27.0 Turn RIGHT onto MA-32A at Hardwick common. *Supplies and restrooms available at Hardwick General Store.* OPTION: Turn left onto MA-32 and follow option directions.

37.1 Continue STRAIGHT through intersection onto Hardwick Road.

37.3 Bear RIGHT at triangle onto Spring Street.

37.6 Turn LEFT onto South Main Street.

37.8 Turn RIGHT onto East Street. *Supplies available at Petersham Country Store.*

41.0 East Street becomes Old Barre Road.

42.3 Old Barre Road becomes Pleasant Street.

45.6 Turn LEFT at stop sign onto MA-32/122.

45.7 Return to Barre town center.

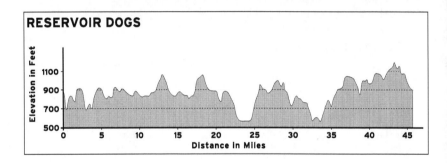

8 WACHUSETT MOUNTAIN   BEST C

Wachusett Mountain State Reservation

**PAVED ROADS WITH SOME DETERIORATING PAVEMENT,
MINIMAL TRAFFIC**

Difficulty: 5   **Total Distance:** 20.1 miles

Riding Time: 2.5 hours   **Elevation Gain:** 1,260 feet

Summary: An uphill battle with incredibly scenic payoffs, this forested ride climbs in the state's rural midsection.

The high point of this ride, both figuratively and geographically, is the summit of Wachusett Mountain, which peaks at 2,006 feet. Some might say the low point is the climb, which is long and slow and hurts. The truth is, it's so beautiful you barely notice the pain.

At least, that's what you should keep telling yourself. That, and that the reason you're panting so hard is not because you're out of shape but because the views are breathtaking.

Wachusett Mountain Ski Area is based at the foot of the mountain, and that's where this ride begins. As you climb, you'll have a chance to crisscross the ski trails, beneath the chairlifts, but first you've got to get there.

The ride heads away from the mountain to start, winding lazily past quiet Noyes Pond and crossing Mare Meadow Reservoir and around the back of the mountain

© CHRIS BERNARD

While you don't want to tackle this ride unless you're willing to climb – a lot – those who do will find the rewards, including the views, worth the effort.

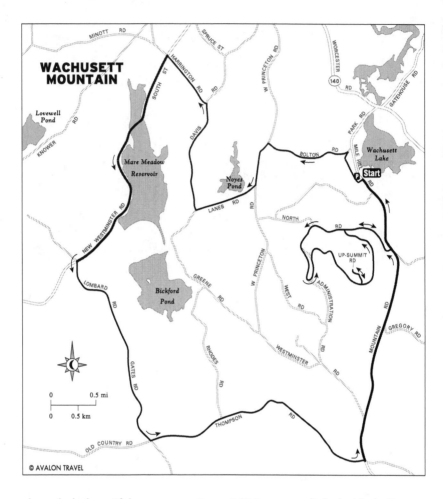

through the beautiful state reservation, a 3,000-acre gem linked with the Leominster State Forest, the Wachusett Meadow Wildlife Sanctuary, and the Minns Wildlife Sanctuary. Some of the trees you'll pass are more than 350 years old.

You get a quick reprieve of a short downhill to the entrance of the reservation before you begin climbing for real up the summit road. Looking down the slopes of the ski area, you'll see the Boston skyline, the Berkshire Mountains, numerous lakes and meadows, and on a clear day, even New Hampshire's Mount Monadnock in the distance. Catch your breath at the visitors center at the summit before descending quickly—and gratefully—back to the start.

Note that the summit road is open from Memorial Day through the last

Sunday in October, 9 A.M.–sunset daily. For more information, contact the Department of Conservation and Recreation at Mountain Road, Princeton, MA 01541, 978/464-2987, www.mass.gov/dcr/parks/central/wach.htm.

Options

Gluttons for punishment can do this ride backward, frontloading two big climbs and making the rest of the ride more or less uphill. This ride is within an hour's drive of Reservoir Dogs.

Locals' Tip: The 1761 Old Mill (69 State Road East, Westminster, MA 01473, 978/874-5941, www.1761oldmill.com) is a rustic restaurant open Tuesday through Sunday, serving locally brewed Wachusett Brewing Company beers.

Places to Stay: The Maguire House bed-and-breakfast (30 Cobb Road, Ashburnham, MA 01430, 978/827-5053, www.maguirehouse.com) is an upscale B&B, built in 1764 and located not far from the ride, with a great location and access to trails and hikes.

Driving Directions

Take MA-2 to exit 25 for Westminster/Princeton. Take MA-140 south, and turn right onto Mile Hill Road. The entrance to the ski area is a half mile down on the right; this ride starts and ends there. Supplies are available in the summer (9 A.M.–5 P.M. Mon.–Fri.).

Route Directions

0.0 From the parking area, exit to the right side of the lot and turn LEFT onto Bolton Road, uphill.

1.3 Turn LEFT onto West Princeton Road, still heading uphill.

1.8 Turn RIGHT onto Lanes Road as the road levels out.

2.4 Turn RIGHT onto Davis Road.

3.7 Turn LEFT onto Harrington Road.

4.5 Turn LEFT onto South Street, cross the Mare Meadow Reservoir, and then follow its shoreline. South Street becomes New Westminster Road and begins a slight downhill.

7.1 Turn LEFT onto Lombard Road. This rural road climbs gradually but steadily through the state reservation.

9.3 Turn LEFT onto Thompson Road.

12.0 Turn LEFT onto Mountain Road, beginning a short downhill to the beginning of the climb.

13.0 Begin the climb.

14.4 Turn LEFT to enter the reservation and follow Up-Summit Road. *The visitors center is on your left.* From here, the climb steepens, but the views improve. The road crosses ski area trails, with chairlifts overhead, and the views to your right go from stunning to breathtaking.

15.8 Follow signs for the summit, bearing RIGHT on Up-Summit Road.

16.2 Stay LEFT on Up-Summit Road, ignoring closed administrative road.

16.5 Stay RIGHT on Up-Summit Road.

17.2 Sharp LEFT to summit.

17.4 Summit! Turn around and bear LEFT onto Down-Summit Road, beginning descent.

18.6 Turn RIGHT onto two-way Summit Road.

19.3 Turn LEFT onto Mountain Road, watching for traffic.

20.1 Turn LEFT into parking area at ski area.

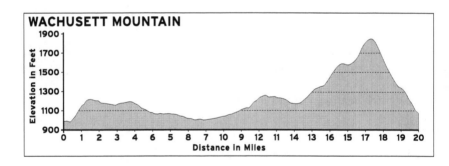

9 NASHUA RIVER RAIL TRAIL BEST ☾
Ayer to Dunstable

PAVED RAIL TRAIL

Difficulty: 2	**Total Distance:** 22.2 miles
Riding Time: 2 hours	**Elevation Gain:** 108 feet

Summary: This smooth, wide, flat rail trail along the river is a wonderful way to spend a day and is suitable for all riders.

Like many other rail trails, the Nashua River trail is flat and easy to ride. But this one is exceptional in ways not easy to quantify. For one thing, it's beautiful along its length from the New Hampshire border south to Ayer. It's also smoothly paved and 10 feet wide, making it safe and accessible to broad groups of users—including equestrians, who get their own five-foot-wide path paralleling 7 miles of the rail trail.

The trail also offers opportunities to stop and rest along the way, to watch for wildlife, and to take pictures—or just take in the sights—at dozens of scenic overlooks and viewpoints. It's tough to find anything to complain about.

Originally the Hollis Branch of the Boston & Maine railroad, this rail trail was completed in 2002, 20 years after the last train used the tracks. The route's usefulness for transportation continues. The trailhead in Ayer is accessible from

© LISA BERNARD

Running south from the New Hampshire border, the Nashua River Rail Trail is wide, smooth, paved, and beautiful.

commuter rail service between Boston and Fitchburg, a move toward a more hopeful future when more bicycle commuting infrastructure is in place.

Flat and smooth as this trail is, it's suitable for bicyclists of all skill levels on any kind of bicycle. Facilities are available at the Ayer trailhead, and you'll find water faucets in front of Groton Town Hall, just off the trail on Station Avenue; watch for signs. Bicyclists should yield to horses on approach and give a verbal acknowledgement before passing.

For more information, contact the Department of Conservation and Recreation, www.mass.gov/dcr/parks/northeast/nash.htm.

Options

Distances are painted on the pavement, so it's easy to piece together a ride of any length—it's all up to you. Additional parking areas can be found along the length of the trail in Groton Center on Court Street, on Groton Sand Hill Road, or in Dunstable on Hollis Street

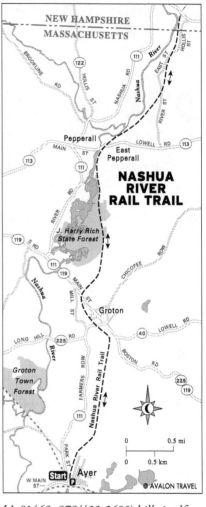

Locals' Tip: Charlotte's Cozy Kitchen (142 Main Street, Pepperell, MA 01463, 978/433-2693) bills itself as the "rail trail's ice cream stop," and in fact, many trail users do take advantage of its proximity. Charlotte's offers other foods as well, and it's a good place to stop for lunch.

Places to Stay: The Ayer Motor Inn (18 Fitchburg Road, Ayer, MA 01432, 978/772-0797) is a bed on a budget—clean, comfortable, and reasonably priced.

Driving Directions

The Ayer trailhead has more parking than the Dunstable end, so start there. From MA-2, take exit 38B, then follow MA-111 north to the rotary in Ayer. Enter the traffic circle at 6 o'clock and exit at 12 o'clock onto Washington Street (MA-2A). Turn right after Ayer Center and take first right on Groton Street. The parking lot is on the right. Additional parking areas along the trail's length can be found in Groton center on Court Street, on Groton Sand Hill Road, or in Dunstable on Hollis Street.

Route Directions

0.0 Head north on the rail trail.

3.1 Trail parking at Groton Center. *Water available.*

4.8 Trail parking at Sand Hill Road in Groton. Trail runs along the J. Harry Rich State Forest, with scenic views.

11.1 Trail ends at Dunstable parking. TURN AROUND.

22.2 END at parking area.

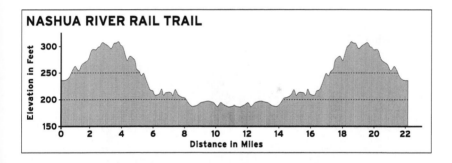

NASHUA RIVER RAIL TRAIL

10 GREAT BROOK FARM TOUR
Great Brook Farm State Park, Carlisle

SINGLE-TRACK, DOUBLE-TRACK, DIRT AND GRAVEL ROADS

Difficulty: 2	**Total Distance:** 9 miles
Riding Time: 1.5-2 hours	**Elevation Gain:** 226 feet

Summary: These shaded, family-friendly mountain bike trails crisscross a state park on the site of a dairy farm.

Locals know there's plenty of good mountain biking to be found within spitting distance of Boston, but Great Brook Farm may not be the first place they think of. For one thing, the trails aren't the primary reason the park is popular—that honor goes to the working dairy farm and its attendant ice-cream stand, the duck ponds and picnic areas, the canoe launch, the cross-country ski touring center, and other family-friendly opportunities. For another, the trails seem to be more well-known among the equestrian crowd than the biking crowd.

But the truth is, the trails here are excellent for mountain biking—in fact, they're maintained by the very active New England Mountain Biking Association (NEMBA)—and are nontechnical enough to be welcoming to even the least-confident off-road riders. This is a great place for beginners.

This ride follows the trails through the woods around Great Brook Farm, but the roads make for popular, bucolic rides as well.

© CHRIS BERNARD

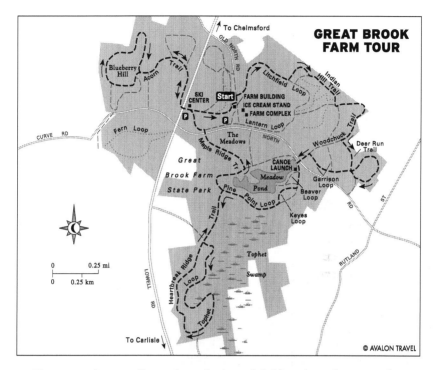

This route takes you all over the park, through fields and meadows, pine forests and woodlands, and past swamps and cornfields. You'll start in the fields, do a little rocky, hilly stretch along the Indian Hill Trail, and ride along some gentle hills on the Woodchuck Trail. It's mostly double- and single-track, but not technical, on this northern side. Across the road, in the southern part of the park, you can find more challenging single-track.

Heartbreak Ridge and Tophet Loop run through the woods along a ridge and past a swamp. The trails are banked nicely to let you gather some speed, and a bridge makes it passable even in wetter seasons. The swamp means mosquitoes, so spray yourself or grit your teeth and bear it.

An easy ride along cornfields brings you to the ski center, where you can cross Lowell Road and take a loop around Blueberry Hill. It's mostly dirt roads and double-track, with a small, more challenging section of single-track that's only hilly and rooty for a short time.

Note that the trails are closed to bikes from December 15 to March 15 and whenever four or more inches of snow cover them. Mountain bikes are the best bet on these trails.

For more information, contact Great Brook Farm State Park, 984 Lowell Road, Carlisle, MA 01741, 978/369-6312, www.state.ma.us/dem/parks/gbfm.htm.

Options

Riders looking for a longer ride can piece together a 5-mile loop around the area by following North Road from Lowell Road east to Rutland Street and turning right. When Rutland Street ends, turn right again on East Street, and right again on Lowell Road to return to the start. The roads are rural and lightly used, and the scenery is beautiful and shaded.

Locals' Tip: If you're riding during the right season, get the ice-cream on site at the stand and general store (984 Lowell Road, Carlisle, MA 01741), where you can see the dairy cows responsible on the premises.

Places to Stay: Concord's Colonial Inn (48 Monument Square, Concord, MA 01742, 978/369-9200, www.concordscolonialinn.com) is a short drive from Great Brook Farm and situated in historic Concord.

Driving Directions

From Lowell, take I-495 to exit 34 and follow MA-110 south for 2.5 miles, to the center of Chelmsford. Follow signs through the one-way system to MA-4 south. Drive 1 mile and bear right onto Concord Road (which becomes Lowell Road). Drive approximately 2.5 miles and turn left onto North Road; look for signs to Great Brook Farm State Park. Turn left into the first parking lot. At the end of this lot, there's a small park building with full facilities, restrooms, water, and trail maps (the main farm building and ice-cream stand are past the pond at the next parking area). The parking fee is $2. The route begins behind this farm building. Supplies and a bike shop are available in Chelmsford.

Route Directions

0.0 START at rear of park building on Litchfield Loop.

0.2 Turn LEFT at fork onto single-track.

0.6 Turn LEFT at edge of field.

0.8 Take the leftmost trail at the three-way intersection onto Indian Hill Trail.

0.9 Turn LEFT onto main trail.

1.2 Stay STRAIGHT through two four-way intersections.

1.3 Cross first bridge and take leftmost trail.

1.6 Turn LEFT at three-way intersection.

1.9 Turn LEFT at four-way intersection.

2.2 Bear RIGHT at junction.

2.3 Turn LEFT at four-way intersection.

2.4 Cross bridge.

2.5 Bear RIGHT on Garrison Loop.

2.8 Turn LEFT onto wide dirt road (Woodchuck Trail, unmarked).

2.9 Cross North Road and pick up Pine Point Loop trail to left of pond.

3.0 OPTION: Take a short, optional side loop left on the Beaver Loop trail.

3.1 Turn LEFT onto Keyes Loop.

3.6 Turn RIGHT back onto Pine Point Loop.

3.9 Turn LEFT onto Heartbreak Ridge trail.

4.2 Turn LEFT at triangular intersection, then make an immediate LEFT onto Tophet Loop trail.

5.0 Turn RIGHT back onto Heartbreak Ridge trail.

5.6 Turn RIGHT at triangular intersection.

5.9 Turn LEFT onto Pine Point Loop.

6.2 Turn LEFT onto Maple Ridge trail.

6.4 Turn LEFT at fork.

6.5 Cross North Road and pick up trail just to the left.

6.7 Arrive at ski touring center parking lot. Cross Lowell Road.

6.8 Pick up Acorn Trail.

7.0 Turn LEFT at fork.

7.3 Turn LEFT at junction on narrow trail.

7.4 Stay STRAIGHT (Acorn South trail goes off to left).

8.2 Turn LEFT at junction onto trail between fields

8.3 Bear LEFT.

8.7 Cross North Road.

8.8 Go through the parking lot and pick up dirt road to left of kiosk.

9.0 END at parking lot.

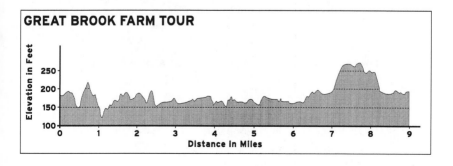

GREAT BROOK FARM TOUR

 11 FARMS AND FORESTS   BEST (

North Andover, Boxford, and Topsfield

PAVED ROADS, MINIMAL TRAFFIC

Difficulty: 2	**Total Distance:** 27.3 miles
Riding Time: 2 hours	**Elevation Gain:** 364 feet

Summary: A flat, winding route through the shady back roads of northeast Massachusetts, with scenic vistas of ponds and forests.

This ride starts and ends at Smolak Farms, a unique and historic spot in the rural fringe of North Andover. The farm stand is a popular meeting spot for local group rides. The lion's share of the farmland is now preserved in cooperation with the state's Agricultural Preservation Restriction Program, which means it will never be developed. The working farm has been around in one form or another for as long as 300 years.

North Andover itself has been around a lot longer—some evidence shows the area has been inhabited for as long as 8,000 years as a Native American encampment, based around Lake Cochichewick. Later, the town was famously sold to a Reverend John Woodbridge for "six pounds and a coat." The town continued to play a part in history—more of its residents were accused of witchcraft during the Salem Witch Trials than residents of the Salem area, and in the 1800s it was home to cotton mills during the textile revolution.

Now it's a town of soccer fields and minivans, but Smolak Farms provides a sense of what the land might once have looked like. This ride heads east on rural, tree-lined roads into Boxford and Topsfield, passing a number of picturesque ponds and lakes, before winding its way clockwise into the verdant Boxford and Harold Parker State Forests. The last stretch passes Lake Cochichewick before arriving through the backdoor at Smolak Farms.

Most of the ride is flat, and there are ample opportunities to stop for snacks or a breather or just to enjoy the archetypal wooded New England setting.

For more information, contact Smolak Farms, 315 South Bradford Street, North Andover, MA 01845, 978/682-6332, www.smolakfarms.com.

Options

To extend this ride by about 15 miles, turn left at Mile 5.8 on Pond Street and right on Killam Hill Road, which becomes Ipswich Road. Bear left onto Boxford Street, which becomes Linebrook Road and skirts the edges of Willowdale State Forest in Ipswich. When Linebrook Road ends, turn right onto MA-133/MA-1A, and

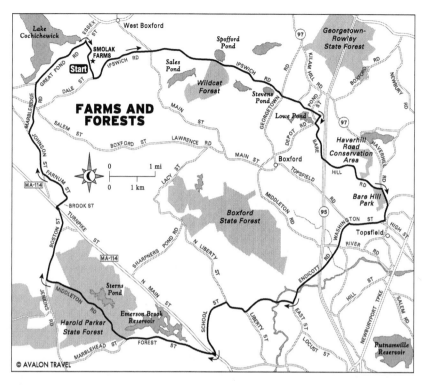

then right onto Market Street/Topsfield Road. Topsfield Road becomes Ipswich Road and rejoins the original ride at Mile 9.

This ride is near the Harold Parker State Forest and Weeping Willowdale off-road rides; combining one or more rides offers a mix of cycling terrain. Witches to Water's Edge, another scenic road ride, is just a half-hour drive away.

Locals' Tip: All the local group rides that start and end at Smolak Farms can't be wrong. Begin your day with a cup of their coffee and a fresh farmhouse doughnut, and end it with pressed apple cider.

Places to Stay: The Killam Hill Cottage (168 Killam Hill Road, Boxford, MA 01921, 978/887-6470) offers no-frills country guest rooms with shared kitchenettes and bathrooms for affordable rates less than a minute from the ride.

Driving Directions

From I-95, take exit 53B for Georgetown/MA-97 north, and turn right at the off-ramp. Take your first left, following the sign for Boxford Village, and take your first right onto Ipswich Road. About 6 miles down, turn right onto South

Bradford Street, following signs for Smolak Farms. A small parking area is available, as are seasonal facilities.

Route Directions

0.0 From the farm parking lot, turn LEFT onto South Bradford Street and LEFT onto Dale Street.

1.0 Stay STRAIGHT on Dale Street, which becomes Ipswich Road (Boxford).

3.5 Pass Spofford Pond on your left. *Take the next left onto Spofford Road to access the pond.*

4.8 Pass Stevens Pond on your right. *A small parking area with water access is available.*

5.8 OPTION: Turn LEFT on Pond Street and follow option directions.

5.9 When road ends, turn RIGHT onto Pond Street and RIGHT onto Depot Road.

6.1 Turn LEFT onto Bare Hill Road.

7.0 Pass over I-95.

8.5 At Bare Hill Park, turn RIGHT onto MA-97/Haverhill Road/ Main Street, past Pine Grove Cemetery.

9.3 Turn RIGHT onto Washington Street (Topsfield).

10.2 Bear LEFT to stay on Washington Street, which becomes Endicott Road.

11.5 Cross over I-95 into Boxford State Forest.

12.5 Turn RIGHT onto Peabody Street.

14.1 Turn LEFT onto School Street.

14.9 School Street ends; turn LEFT onto Essex Street.

15.6 Essex Street ends. Cross MA-114 onto Forest Street. This is a busy road—be careful crossing.

17.6 Forest Street ends. Turn RIGHT onto Salem Street/Middleton Road into Harold Parker State Forest.

20.0 Turn RIGHT onto Jenkins Road/Boston Street (Andover).

21.6 Jenkins Road/Boston Street ends. Turn LEFT onto MA-114. This is a busy road—be careful crossing.

21.7 Turn RIGHT onto Brook Street (North Andover).

22.0 Turn LEFT onto Farnum Street.

22.8 Farnum Street ends. Bear RIGHT onto Johnson Street.

23.9 Turn RIGHT onto Marbleridge Road.

25.0 Bear RIGHT onto Great Pond Road. Lake Cochichewick is on your left.

26.5 Turn RIGHT onto South Bradford Street.

27.3 END at parking area.

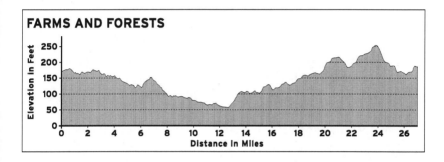

FARMS AND FORESTS

12 HAROLD PARKER STATE FOREST

BEST ☾

Harold Parker State Forest, Andover

SINGLE-TRACK, DOUBLE-TRACK

Difficulty: 2   **Total Distance:** 7.5 miles

Riding Time: 2 hours   **Elevation Gain:** 300 feet

Summary: Enjoy this nontechnical ride through a gorgeous, shady state forest, with opportunities for more intense routes at every turn.

It's possible to piece together 35 miles of riding in Harold Parker State Forest, and the terrain is so well-suited to mountain biking that some of the area's best riders come each year to compete in the "Wicked Ride of the East" race. But the park's real appeal is the seemingly endless winding trails that show off the wooded beauty of Massachusetts's second-oldest state park.

In all, the park covers 3,000 glacially carved acres of rolling hills, grassy wetlands, and rocky outcroppings. Trails range from double-track jeep roads to wooded single-track. This loop is largely nontechnical—the few stretches of

The trails of Harold Parker State Forest are popular with mountain bikers from all over the region.

© CHRIS BERNARD

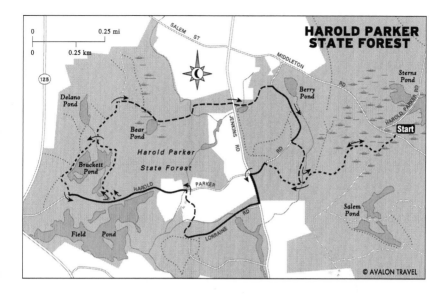

single-track are suitable for beginners who take it slowly, and the entire trail is ideal for cyclocross bikes.

Dense tree cover here prevents much sunlight from reaching parts of the trails, which means they can be muddy in the spring (with snow and ice sometimes lingering) and cool and moist on hot summer days. During the fall, the foliage can be spectacular. Use caution when those leaves end up wet on the ground; they can mask obstacles such as roots or rocks and make trails slippery.

Expect to share the trail with other users, including pedestrians and dog walkers, and be aware that some trails' spurs dead-end into private property. Along the trails, watch for remnants of 18th-century homesteads, sawmills, and stone walls dating back even further. Homes surrounding the forest are said to have been Underground Railroad hideouts, and many still have secret doors and chambers.

For more information on the park, visit the Harold Parker State Forest online at www.mass.gov/dcr/parks/northeast/harp.htm.

Options

For shorter, scenic rides, follow the out-and-back trails around Brackett and Collins Ponds. For more of a challenge, try the three-mile trail in the forest's northernmost section between Middleton and Turnpike Roads (MA-114) or the hilly single-track trails north of Berry Pond.

This ride is near Farms and Forests and Weeping Willowdale. Bicyclists spending a few days in the area might consider combining Harold Parker with the Weeping Willowdale ride for a taste of some of the best state forest trails in the region. Or, put in some road miles on Farms and Forests to give the body a break from the bumps of off-roading.

Locals' Tip: Fuel up for a ride at Harrison's Roast Beef (80 Chickering Road/ MA-125, North Andover, MA 01845, 978/687-9158), a local favorite known for its good food and brusque service.

Places to Stay: Harold Parker State Forest offers nearly 100 well-spread-out campsites, each with picnic table and grill, and with public restrooms with hot water showers, and is open May to mid-October. For more information on the campground, call 978/475-7972.

Driving Directions

From the south, take I-93 north to exit 41. Follow MA-125 north for about 4 miles to the state police barracks on the right. Turn right on Harold Parker Road. Turn left on Jenkins Road and right onto Salem Road, and drive 1.25 miles to forest headquarters, on the left. From the north, take I-495 south to exit 42. Travel east on MA-114 for 6 miles. Take a right at the brown Harold Parker State Forest sign. Follow the road to the end, then take a left to the headquarters.

Route Directions

0.0 START on unpaved road across from park headquarters.

0.3 Turn RIGHT at first fork.

0.5 Turn LEFT at next fork.

1.1 Turn LEFT sharply at gravel parking area onto single-track.

1.2 Turn LEFT on Jenkins Road (paved).

1.4 Turn RIGHT onto paved road into the Lorraine Park campground area.

1.9 Turn RIGHT along the edges of Field Pond.

2.3 Turn LEFT onto Harold Parker Road (paved).

2.5 Turn RIGHT onto double-track. Trail merges with wider, old road.

2.8 Bear LEFT at first fork.

3.0 Bear LEFT at next fork, circumnavigating Brackett and Collins Ponds.

3.4 Turn LEFT onto Harold Parker Road (paved).

3.9 Turn LEFT onto double-track. Merges with wider, old road.

4.2 Turn RIGHT on trail.

5.7 CROSS Jenkins Road (paved).

6.5 Turn RIGHT on Berry Pond Road (paved).

6.7 Turn LEFT onto unpaved road.

7.0 Turn RIGHT at first fork.

7.2 Turn LEFT at next fork.

7.5 END at park headquarters.

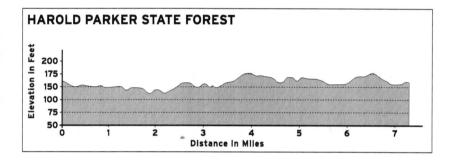

13 WEEPING WILLOWDALE   BEST ❿
Willowdale State Forest, Ipswich

DIRT ROADS, SINGLE-TRACK, DOUBLE-TRACK

Difficulty: 2   **Total Distance:** 6.4 miles

Riding Time: 1 hour   **Elevation Gain:** 102 feet

Summary: Fly along fast, fun cross-country trails and single-track through a shaded, buggy state forest.

Like a lot of state forest trails in this part of Massachusetts, there's a lot of variety in Willowdale. That means riders can pick and choose to their liking, constructing on-the-fly routes that are as fast and challenging or lazy and scenic as they choose.

The fact is, you almost can't go wrong. The forest has no shortage of single-track, which draws experienced mountain bikers from all over the region. In fact, former national cyclocross champions, Massachusetts residents, and husband and wife team Tim Johnson and Lyne Bessette can be seen riding here. You'll find the occasional stunt, but for the most part just well-maintained, nontechnical single-track.

But even the dirt roads and wide double-track are fun here. Ride them at full speed, winding around the corners, or soft pedal your way through the forest

© CHRIS BERNARD

Willowdale State Forest is an appealing mix of single-track and fire roads ideal for a cyclocross bike.

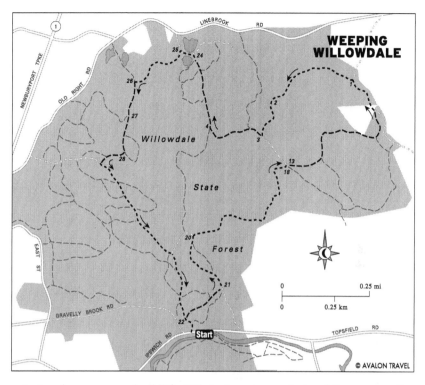

enjoying the swamps and wildlife. Ride in the autumn, during foliage season, for maximum scenic impact. You're not likely to get tired of the rides in Willowdale, but if you do, cross the Ipswich River from your parking area and start all over again exploring the trails at Bradley Palmer State Park.

Ipswich is a beautiful and historic coastal town that seems a world away from the forest on its edge. Just half an hour north of Boston, it's a tourist destination, but Willowdale is a gem that's largely ignored—especially compared to Bradley Palmer. You're likely to encounter a few other bike riders, and the occasional dog walker, but that's it—it's largely, wonderfully uncrowded. You might see riders on horses, but you're more likely to see their leave-behinds, an excellent way to practice your bunny hopping skills on your bike, considering the consequences of failure.

Trails are nominally marked with blazes and signpost numbers, though in reality, markers are faded or missing at many intersections. The forest's not big enough to get truly lost in, however, and riders can always make their way out to one of the roads bordering the woods to find their location.

Mountain bikes and cyclocross bikes are ideal, but recreational riders who stick to the wide, unpaved roads and double-track will do fine on hybrids.

For more information, contact the Department of Conservation and Recreation, 251 Causeway Street, Suite 600, Boston, MA 02114, 617/626-1250, www.mass.gov/dcr.

Options

Extend your ride by following the many trails in the state forest at random, or plan ahead of time using a trail map. Maps of neighboring Bradley Palmer State Park are available at www.mass.gov/dcr/parks/northeast/brad.htm.

Bicyclists in the area should try the Harold Parker State Forest ride, which offers similar trails in the same setting just 45 minutes away. Or, stretch your legs on the roads of the nearby Farms and Forests ride for a varied cycling experience.

Locals' Tip: The Choate Bridge Pub (3 South Main Street, Ipswich, MA 01938, 978/356-2931, www.ipswichma.com) is a comfortable local bar and grill set beside the oldest stone arch bridge in America, built in 1764. Note that the Choate Bridge Pub is cash only.

Places to Stay: The Inn at Castle Hill on the Crane Estate (a property of the trustees of reservations, 280 Argilla Road, Ipswich, MA 01938, 978/412-2555, www.craneestate.org) offers stunning ocean and marsh views from the historic Crane Estate, just a short drive from Willowdale.

Driving Directions

From I-95, take exit 50 to US-1 North. Travel 4 miles and turn right onto Ipswich Road. About 2 miles down, Ipswich Road turns into Topsfield Road. There will be two turn-outs on the right side for parking; park in the second, at the footbridge across the Ipswich River. The ride starts across the street.

Route Directions

0.0 From Ipswich Road, enter the forest at the gate.

0.2 At the intersection at signpost 22, take a RIGHT.

0.4 Turn LEFT at signpost 21 onto an unpaved road.

0.7 Continue right on the fire road at signpost 20.

1.6 Just past signpost 18, turn RIGHT at signpost 13. Bear LEFT at next two forks.

2.4 Turn LEFT on paved road. Ride about a half-mile past the Private Property sign (please respect the homes along the right side of the road).

2.7 Turn LEFT on trail marked by half-buried concrete blocks and signpost 1.

3.3 At the next intersection, signpost 2, turn LEFT, and then RIGHT at signpost 3 onto single-track.

3.9 Turn RIGHT at signpost 4 onto trail marked with white blazes.

4.3 Turn LEFT at signpost 24.

4.4 Turn LEFT at signpost 25.

4.6 Turn LEFT at signpost 26 onto single-track.

4.8 Stay STRAIGHT at signpost 27, and turn RIGHT at signpost 28.

5.3 At the next intersection, turn LEFT on unpaved road (marked with white blazes).

5.9 Bear RIGHT at the next fork onto unpaved road. Stay STRAIGHT past signpost 22, which brings you to Ipswich Road.

6.4 END at parking area.

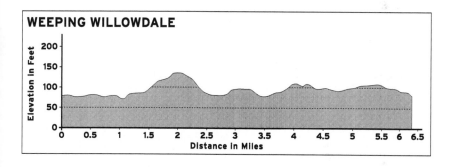

14 PLUM ISLAND BEST (
Parker River National Wildlife Refuge

DIRT ROADS, PAVED ROADS WITH SOME DETERIORATING PAVEMENT AND MODERATE TRAFFIC

Difficulty: 2 | **Total Distance:** 20.6 miles

Riding Time: 2 hours | **Elevation Gain:** 10 feet

Summary: This scenic ride brings you close to the water and nature – and traffic. Plan on parking and walking for up-close sights.

The 11-mile-long barrier island off the coast of northeast Massachusetts, Plum Island, was named as far back as 1649. It probably wasn't long after that when hordes of tourists began visiting it each summer, and these days it can be fairly crowded when the weather's nice. Despite the island's provenance being split between four neighboring towns, access to the island is limited to a single road in from Newburyport.

Packed with restaurants, bars, shops, and galleries, Newburyport is a cool little coastal New England town. Leaving from Market Square, downtown, you'll see a lot of vehicles—both moving and parked on the side of the road—on Water Street, so ride smartly. Once you're out of town, the shoulder of the Plum Island Turnpike provides ample riding room. The route itself is flat, and it travels through salt marshes, past the Plum Island Airport, and eventually across a metal-grated bridge before entering the Parker River National Wildlife Refuge (www.fws.gov/northeast/parkerriver/).

© SARGE BERNARD

This ride through the Parker River National Wildlife Refuge is suitable for riders of all skill levels.

Tourists aren't the only things flocking to the area, which is both good and bad for you. On the good side are the more than 300 species of birds that visit each year. On the other are the nasty, biting greenheads and the mosquitoes that are the banes of the beach come summer. Be prepared from June to August or so to lose a few pounds of flesh.

Sadly, bikes are not allowed on the various hiking trails off the main route, but there are some bike racks available at refuge parking lots, allowing you to explore the many walking trails. Please obey posted signs, as the sand dunes are fragile, and observe restrictions around the breeding grounds of the piping plover. Beaches are closed during plover breeding season, which begins in April

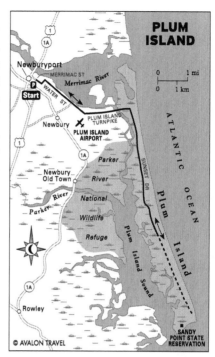

and sometimes goes as late as August. Bring sunscreen, a windbreaker, and warm clothing in the spring and fall as the weather can change pretty quickly.

The road turns to packed dirt and gravel for about 6 miles at the end of the ride. Morning cycling is recommended, before traffic gets unbearable. The refuge entrance fee is $2 (for bikes and walkers). Maps are available at the gatehouse; public restrooms are available at the gatehouse and farther along inside Parker River National Wildlife Refuge.

For more information, contact the Newburyport Chamber of Commerce, 38R Merrimac Street, Newburyport, MA 01950, 978/462-6680, www.newbury portchamber.org.

Options

To add a 7-mile loop through old Newbury and marshland, on the return trip take your first left after the airport onto Ocean Avenue, and then turn left again onto MA-1A south. At the 3-mile mark, turn right onto Newman Road and right again onto Hay Street, which brings you back to MA-1A. Turn left and follow 1A back to turn right on Ocean Avenue, rejoining the ride by turning left on Water Street and returning to the parking area.

Locals' Tip: The Fish Tale Diner (Bridge Marina, US-1 Bridge, Salisbury,

MA 01952, 978/462-2274, www.bridgemarinasalisbury.com) is a great place to dine while watching the boats come and go in the harbor, with great views of the water. Try the Belgian waffles.

Places to Stay: 167 Water B&B (167 Water Street, Newburyport, MA 01950, 978/255-2386, www.167water.com) is as welcoming as a bed-and-breakfast can be, with river views and friendly hosts.

Driving Directions

From US-1, head east on Merrimac Street for about 0.4 mile into downtown Newburyport. Free parking is available in lots throughout Newburyport, though in summer you'll need to stake your claim early in the day, especially on the weekends. The ride starts downtown at Market Square, at the intersection of Merrimac, State, and Water Streets. Supplies and a bike shop are available in Newburyport.

Route Directions

0.0 START from Market Square. Proceed east down Water Street.

0.2 Bear LEFT, continuing down Water Street. (This eventually turns into the Plum Island Turnpike.)

1.4 Pass Massachusetts Audubon Center.

2.9 Cross metal grated bridge.

3.3 Turn RIGHT on Sunset Drive.

3.8 Enter Parker River National Wildlife Refuge. Pay entry fee.

6.3 Bear LEFT.

7.4 Road turns to gravel.

10.3 Enter Sandy Point State Reservation. *Park your bike on the bike rack and walk to the various beaches.* TURN AROUND and retrace your route back to Newburyport. OPTION: Take the first LEFT after the airport onto Ocean Avenue and follow option directions.

20.6 Arrive at Market Square.

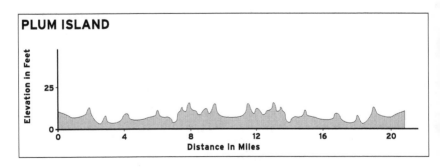

PLUM ISLAND

15 WITCHES TO WATER'S EDGE BEST ℂ
Salem to Cape Ann

PAVED ROADS WITH MODERATE TRAFFIC

Difficulty: 3 **Total Distance:** 54.3 miles

Riding Time: 4 hours **Elevation Gain:** 775 feet

Summary: This mostly flat road ride leaves historic downtown Salem for the scenic coastal routes of Cape Ann.

Originally named Cape Tragbigzanda by explorer John Smith, Cape Ann— renamed by King Charles I—is everything you'd expect of coastal New England. From working-class fishing town Gloucester to upscale Magnolia with its cliff-front mansions, it's scenic and varied. This ride explores enough of it to get a sense of the variety.

Begin south of Cape Ann, in Salem, best known for being historically unwelcoming to witches. Since then, the city has come to embrace its past, and you'll find evidence of that fact in the shops and museums and even along the streets. The first part of the ride is on the busiest roads, in Salem, and across the bridge in Beverly. There aren't shoulders on all the roads, and during rush hour there can be a lot of traffic. The traffic thins out as you go, but it's present on much of this ride—these aren't the rural farm roads of the central and western part of the state—so be warned, and be careful.

© CHRIS BERNARD

This ride starts and ends in historic Salem, birthplace of Nathaniel Hawthorne, and the site of a pro-level criterium bike race that passes the famous Salem Witch Museum.

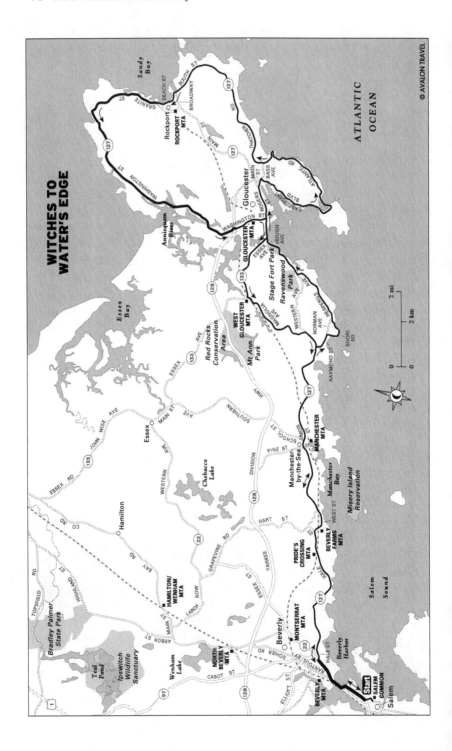

North of Beverly, the ride heads through Pride's Crossing and Beverly Farms, where you'll see lots of big impressive gates hiding big impressive homes. John Updike lived there for years, and you'll bike right past his home. Then the route passes through Manchester-by-the-Sea, a cute little waterfront town, and into Magnolia, where it strays off the main road for a loop along the cliffs, offering stunning views of the ocean and the homes along its edge. You'll also pass the medieval-style castle built by inventor John Hammond, creator of, among other things, the remote control.

From there it's north and east to Gloucester, best known by many as the setting for *The Perfect Storm,* but first made famous a century earlier by Rudyard Kipling in *Captains Courageous.* The ride passes through Stage Fort Park, a beautiful oceanfront park that's the site of one of the country's largest cyclocross races each fall, then out to the Bass Rocks area where, on stormy days, the ocean throws rocks onto the road.

Next, head east to Rockport, a postcard of a coastal town surrounded on three sides by ocean. There, a spur road leads to Motif No. 1, a wharf shack considered the most-painted and photographed building in America. The rest of the ride rolls through the scenic neighborhood of Annisquam and the fringes of Essex, where the fried clam was invented, before retracing part of the route back to Salem.

For more information, contact the Cape Ann Chamber of Commerce, 33 Commercial Street, Gloucester, MA 01930, 978/283-1601, www.capeann vacations.com.

Options

Cut 16 miles of the busiest roads off this ride by parking in downtown Manchester-by-the-Sea and picking up the ride at Mile 8, leaving you with an easier distance, less traffic, and just as much beauty.

Locals' Tip: When not being burned at the stake, Salem residents can be found at Red's Sandwich Shop (15 Central Street, Salem, MA 01970, 978/745-3527, www.redssandwichshop.com), where the diner-type breakfasts are worth waiting for.

Places to Stay: The Cape Ann Motor Inn (33 Rockport Road, Gloucester, MA 01930, 800/464-VIEW, www.capeannmotorinn.com) is an inexpensive place to stay right on Gloucester's Long Beach.

Driving Directions

From MA-128 North, take exit 20B and turn right onto MA-1A toward Beverly. Cross the bridge and turn left onto Pleasant Street, and then bear left at Washington Square at the common. Parking is along the street. The ride starts in front of the Salem Witch Museum at the corner of Hawthorne Boulevard and Brown Street on Washington Square.

Route Directions

0.0 From the Salem Witch Museum, turn LEFT onto Hawthorne Boulevard/MA-1A, and then turn RIGHT at Bridge Street to stay on MA-1A. Follow MA-1A across the bridge into Beverly.

1.3 Immediately after the bridge, bear RIGHT onto Cabot Street/MA-22.

2.1 Turn RIGHT onto Hale Street, which becomes MA-62.

2.6 Stay on Hale Street, which becomes MA-127.

4.3 Along the ocean, Hale Street passes Endicott College on the left.

5.5 Enter Pride's Crossing. Be careful crossing the train tracks.

6.0 Enter Beverly Farms.

7.5 Turn RIGHT onto Boardman Avenue for a short loop out to Tucks Point. After turning around at Tucks Point, turn RIGHT onto Harbor Street and RIGHT onto MA-127, rejoining the ride at Mile 7.8.

8.5 Stay on MA-127. Pass through downtown Manchester-by-the-Sea. *Bike shop and supplies available.*

11.4 Turn RIGHT onto Raymond Street.

11.9 Turn RIGHT onto Shore Road along the cliffs of Magnolia. Shore Road becomes Hesperus Avenue.

13.8 Pass Hammond Castle Museum.

14.5 Turn RIGHT onto MA-127.

15.3 Turn RIGHT onto Hough Avenue, entering Gloucester's Stage Fort Park.

15.6 Turn RIGHT onto MA-127, exiting the park.

17.4 Turn RIGHT onto East Main Street, which becomes Eastern Point Boulevard, loops along Wonson Cove, Lighthouse Cove, Niles Pond, and Brace Cove, and then becomes Atlantic Road.

22.7 Turn RIGHT onto Bass Rocks Road, then RIGHT again onto Atlantic Road.

23.2 Stay STRAIGHT onto MA-127A/Thatcher Road into Rockport.

27.8 Turn RIGHT onto Bearskin Neck Road out to Bradley Wharf to see Motif No. 1. Turn around.

28.2 Turn RIGHT onto Main Street, then bear RIGHT again onto Beach Street past the Old Parish Cemetery on your left.

28.8 Bear RIGHT onto MA-127/Granite Street past Pigeon Cove, Folly Cove, and Halibut Point State Park. *Picnic tables and restrooms available.*

34.0 Pass Lobster Cove on your right, and then Goose Cove on your left.

36.8 Enter traffic circle at 6 o'clock and exit at 12 o'clock onto Washington Street. (Watch for traffic.)

37.8 Turn RIGHT onto Middle Street, and then RIGHT again onto MA-127/Western Avenue.

38.1 Before Stage Fort Park, bear RIGHT onto MA-133/Essex Avenue.

40.0 Turn LEFT onto Magnolia Avenue.

42.2 Turn RIGHT onto MA-127/Western Avenue/Summer Street. Stay on MA-127, retracing the route into Beverly.

51.7 Bear RIGHT onto Hale Street/MA-22.

52.1 Turn LEFT onto Cabot Street/MA-22.

52.8 Merge with MA-1A and cross the bridge into Salem.

53.9 Turn LEFT to stay on MA-1A.

54.3 END at Salem Witch Museum.

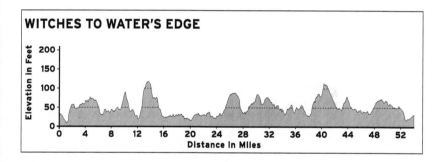

WITCHES TO WATER'S EDGE

16 VIETNAM SAMPLER   BEST (

Milford

SINGLE-TRACK, DIRT ROADS

Difficulty: 3	**Total Distance:** 6.8 miles
Riding Time: 1.5 hours	**Elevation Gain:** 250 feet

Summary: Explore some of the best purpose-built mountain bike trails in New England.

The New England Mountain Bike Association (NEMBA) made history in 2003 when it purchased 47 acres of land in Milford and set it aside for nonmotorized vehicles. Land ownership comes with challenges—for one thing, the parcel is largely "landlocked," meaning NEMBA relies on adjacent property owners to allow cyclists to access the land—and the group has been working diligently to meet them.

With NEMBA working to balance trail-building with land stewardship, all while remaining good neighbors, everyone who uses the trails must be on board with the group's mission. The 47-acre parcel connects with nearly 1,000 acres of non-NEMBA–owned land, so it's important to obey land-use and property boundary signs. Please respect property rights.

Now that the caveats are out of the way, on to the good stuff—the trails in this lot, known as "Vietnam," are among the best purpose-built mountain bike trails in New England. They range from fire roads to single-track, covering everything

NEMBA's bike trail-specific property, known informally as Vietnam, is a mountain biker's playground and paradise.

from slick rock to mud pits to ledges in between. You'll find obstacles to overcome, turns to navigate, short climbs to ascend, jumps to take, and endless hours of fun.

If there's a downside to the area, it's that trails are not well-marked—or, in most cases, marked at all. Perhaps the best way to learn the lay of the land is to join up with an informal guide through the NEMBA membership forum (www.nemba.org) or to ask to join a group of riders at the trails. Rough trail maps are available on the website, as well.

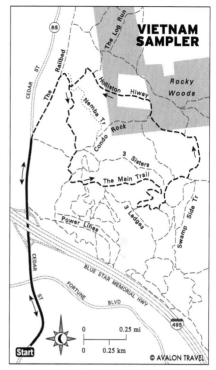

That said, there's nothing wrong with just exploring the area on your own. Trails are easy to find, and they're all fun. Allow yourself plenty of time, and if you have a GPS unit or compass to help yourself find your way back out, all the better. Note that when entering the land, you'll pass several trailheads that are not legal NEMBA access points. Please follow the route directions.

For more information, contact the New England Mountain Bike Association, P.O. Box 2221, Acton, MA 01720, 978/635-1718, www.nemba.org.

Options

With 47 acres of trails and new routes being added or improved all the time, it's possible to return to Vietnam as often as you want without being bored. The route cited here is just a sampler, and it crosses dozens of other networked trails. Riders wishing to lengthen their route or make it more or less challenging should have no trouble doing so.

Locals' Tip: The Alamo (55 Medway Road, Milford, MA 01757, 508/482-0030, http://thealamomexicano.com) is a themed Mexican restaurant that offers a decent, affordable way to end a good day riding Vietnam. Clean the mud off your shoes first, please.

Places to Stay: A half dozen hotels are within biking distance of Vietnam, and you pass every one of them on the route described here, including the Fairfield Inn and Suites (1 Fortune Boulevard, Milford, MA 01757, 508/478-0900).

Driving Directions

From I-495, take exit 20 for MA-85 toward Hopkinton. After about a quarter of a mile, turn right onto Cedar Street. The parking area is on your right, after the cemetery, at Hayward Field.

Route Directions

0.0 From the parking area, turn LEFT onto MA-85/Cedar Street. Traffic can be heavy here, so stick to the shoulder.

1.2 Enter trails via the Railbed on the right side of the road.

1.6 At the first intersection, turn RIGHT onto an unmarked trail.

1.8 Bear RIGHT at the next intersection onto Charles River Trail (unmarked).

2.3 Bear RIGHT at the next intersection, and then LEFT, then RIGHT.

2.6 Bear LEFT at the next intersection onto the Main Trail (unmarked), staying on this trail past the next turn.

3.3 At the intersection, turn RIGHT, and wind your way past the giant, glacially formed rockpile known informally as Teetering Rock.

3.6 At the next three intersections, turn LEFT.

3.9 Bear RIGHT at the next two intersections.

4.2 Turn LEFT, and then LEFT again.

5.0 At the next major intersection of trails, turn LEFT, and stay on this trail until it rejoins the Railbed.

5.2 Turn LEFT on the Railbed.

5.6 Turn LEFT onto Cedar Street.

6.8 END at parking area.

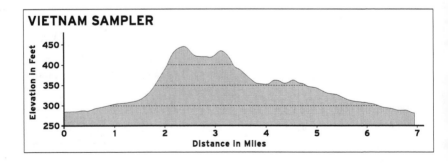

17 TRAIL OF TEARS
West Barnstable Conservation Area

SINGLE-TRACK

Difficulty: 4   **Total Distance:** 12 miles

Riding Time: 2.5 hours   **Elevation Gain:** 302 feet

Summary: Miles of fun, twisting single-track winds its way through deep scrub pine and oak forest.

The West Barnstable Conservation Area is an oasis in the midst of a desert of traffic on a hot summer day. As the cars line up for miles upon miles, bumper to bumper, waiting to get to Cape Cod destinations, smart cyclists are already on the trails of this 1,000-plus-acre conservation area that offers some of the best mountain biking in the state.

The trails aren't particularly technical, but they'll challenge your aerobic fitness on the short, steep ascents and descents. One minute you're in low gear puffing up a hill, and the next minute you're bouncing off rocks down a steep slope. Most of the time, though, you're twisting through soft pine-covered trails, sliding between slender tree trunks and wondering which way to turn at the upcoming fork in the trail.

This is really fun riding, great for intermediate riders who want a break from the rocky, muddy trails of New England's interior.

A designated 16-mile single-track Trail of Tears is signposted with red and white mile markers. It's not always easy to follow, and up-to-date trail maps are hard to come by. It seems as if new paths are being created all the time, and it's very easy to get lost. There are three types of markers—the red and white Trail of Tears signs, brown signs with white arrows, and small circular patches with reflective arrows. In general, the best bet is to follow what appears to be the main trail—it's usually a little

The Trail of Tears offers Cape Cod cyclists a single-track break from the often-crowded beachfront roads and rail trails.

© CHRIS BERNARD

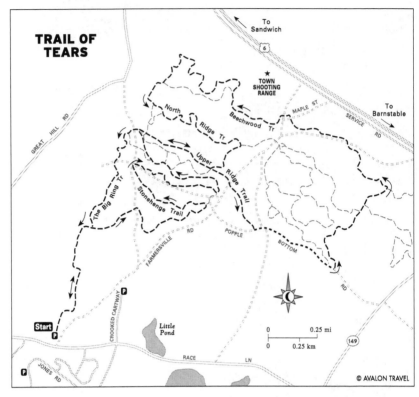

sandier and more packed down. Newer trails are more loamy and have more pine coverage.

This route follows most of the Trail of Tears, starting on some tight single-track with some fun downs and ups on the way to the Walker Point lookout platform. A few rocky patches mix in with the pine trails as you work your way east. The northeast corner is more sandy and you'll ride parallel to the power lines until returning to deeper, leafier forested areas in the northwest corner. Bring a GPS unit if you have one, and be prepared to get lost.

For more information and to obtain a trail map, contact the Barnstable Conservation Commission, 200 Main Street, Hyannis, MA 02601, 508/862-4093, www.town.barnstable.ma.us.

Options

To extend this ride, take a sharp left around Mile 5.8 onto a single-track, called the Broken Arrow Trail, which crisscrosses an area known as the Field of Dreams.

At marker 7.4 turn right, then left at Mile 8.2 to rejoin the main route directions at Mile 6.2.

Locals' Tip: Barnstable Restaurant and Tavern (3176 Main Street, Barnstable, MA 02630, 508/362-235, www.barnstablerestaurant.com) is a local cornerstone, well worth a visit.

Places to Stay: The staff at the Lamb and Lion (2504 Main Street, West Barnstable, MA 02668, 508/362-6823, www.lambandlion.com) bills it as the warmth of an award-winning Cape Cod inn with the spirit of a small luxury hotel. See if they're right.

Driving Directions

From points east and west, take MA-6 to exit 5, MA-149. Drive south on MA-149 for about 1.5 miles; at the intersection, turn right onto Race Lane. Drive 1.8 miles and turn right onto Farmersville Road. Look for the sign for West Barnstable Conservation Area. A gravel parking lot is large enough for about a dozen cars. A trail map is posted at the trailhead, and there is a white Trail of Tears marker. There are no facilities here or at the other two parking lots for the conservation area. Supplies can be found in West Barnstable, Barnstable, and Hyannis; the closest bike shops are in Hyannis.

Route Directions

0.0 START from parking lot.

0.7 Turn RIGHT at the T junction.

0.8 Turn RIGHT at the fork.

1.0 Stay STRAIGHT across the intersection (with wider dirt track) onto single-track.

1.7 Turn LEFT at the intersection.

2.2 Come to a five-way intersection. Look for the single-track going STRAIGHT across the intersection, across a dirt road.

2.8 Turn LEFT at junction.

3.2 Continue STRAIGHT past Spur 2 and Spur 1.

3.4 Arrive at Walker Point lookout platform (you'll see a 3.4-mile marker).

3.4 Continue STRAIGHT at next marker (ignore two trails on left).

3.4 Cross a paved road and turn LEFT, then immediately RIGHT.

3.5 Come to a four-way intersection and go RIGHT (this is marked as a three-way intersection on most trail maps; the newest trail is the one straight ahead). At the next intersection, go RIGHT (ignore small trail on left).

3.6 Continue STRAIGHT at marker, uphill.

4.1 Come to a five-way intersection and go STRAIGHT across (ignore one trail on left and two trails on right; this is marked as a four-way intersection on most trail maps).

4.2 Turn RIGHT onto road, then make an immediate LEFT onto single-track trail.

4.5 Cross road, go STRAIGHT.

4.7 Cross road, go STRAIGHT.

4.9 Turn LEFT at fork and continue STRAIGHT on main trail, ignoring side trails.

5.2 Turn RIGHT onto wide trail.

5.3 Turn LEFT onto dirt road.

5.8 OPTION: Sharp LEFT onto a Broken Arrow Trail and follow the option directions.

6.0 Turn LEFT off wide path onto single-track.

6.2 Go under power lines.

6.3 Stay STRAIGHT across dirt road.

6.7 Turn RIGHT at fork in trail, follow signs.

7.1 Turn LEFT at Trail of Tears sign (marked 11.8).

7.8 Turn LEFT at intersection.

7.8 Turn LEFT at fork.

8.0 Turn RIGHT at intersection.

8.5 Turn LEFT at intersection.

8.7 Trail loops to RIGHT following trail marker.

8.8 Turn LEFT at intersection with wider trail.

8.9 Go STRAIGHT under power lines.

8.9 Turn LEFT back onto single-track trail.

9.0 Turn LEFT at fork.

9.1 Turn LEFT (carrying on main trail).

9.8 Turn RIGHT at fork.

10.0 Turn RIGHT at the five-way intersection.

10.5 Continue STRAIGHT at the four-way intersection, then RIGHT at fork.

10.6 Turn LEFT uphill at fork.

10.8 Continue STRAIGHT across dirt road.

10.9 Follow arrow to RIGHT.

11.2 Turn RIGHT at intersection, then LEFT at unmarked trail to go back to parking lot. (Don't miss this turn!)

12.0 Return to parking lot.

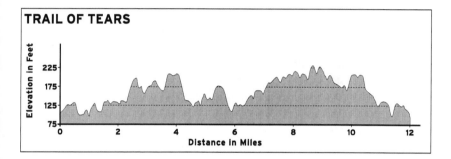

TRAIL OF TEARS

18 CAPE COD RAIL TRAIL
South Dennis to Wellfleet

PAVED BIKE PATH

Difficulty: 2

Riding Time: 5 hours

Total Distance: 44 miles

Elevation Gain: 398 feet

Summary: A well-thought-out and well-used paved trail cutting through the heart of Cape Cod, this ride will please everyone.

When you think Cape Cod, what do you think of? Maybe it's the beaches or the islands. Maybe it's the seafood, or the fishing, or whale watching. Maybe it's the Kennedys. If you've been to the Cape during the summer season, chances are good you also think of the traffic—there's one main road to and from the Cape, and it's well traveled.

Similarly, the beaches can be crowded, and the small towns, while delightful, can also frustrate with their lines and the people milling about from shop to shop and restaurant to restaurant.

This trail is not immune to those crowds, and it can get busy with cyclists, walkers, joggers, and other trail users, but it will nevertheless offer some respite from the masses—especially if you choose your time to ride wisely. Mornings the

© CHRIS BERNARD

The Cape Cod Rail Trail is well-marked and well-traveled, and provides a safe ride along a good length of the Cape on more than 20 miles of scenic bike path.

trail is slow to fill, and weekdays seem better than weekends. Best of all is the off-season, either late spring or early fall, before the weather turns.

Stretching 22 miles from South Dennis to Wellfleet, this trail is paved and flat throughout. Turn around whenever you like to shorten it, or spend a lazy day exploring its length. You'll find plenty of places to stop and explore as you go. Just 3.2 miles in to the trail, you'll come to a unique feature—a rotary, or traffic circle, for bicycles, where the Cape Cod Rail Trail meets the 8-mile Harwich-Chatham rail trail. In the center of the rotary, a grassy area contains picnic tables and bike racks, a signboard shows maps of the trails, and the trails intersect without difficulty thanks to the roundabout traffic flow.

To shorten the trip, start at Nickerson State Park, which also makes a good rest stop about halfway along the trail. Bike rental shops are at many points along the route if you don't have your own bike with you. (The park also offers mountain bike trails.)

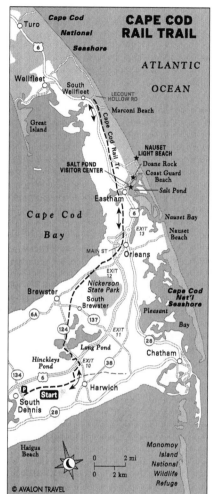

Along the route, you'll pass by the shores of Swan Pond, cross many roads, and ride through a few tunnels. You'll find a string of pretty ponds, all of which look inviting for swimming. After some suburban scenery, there's a scenic stretch of typical Cape lowland scrub pine forest, interrupted briefly by the town of Brewster. On either side of Orleans, you'll ride through marshlands, which offer birding opportunities.

Just before the turnaround point, you'll pass an opportunity for a side trip to Marconi National Seashore. The trail ends off LeCount Hollow Road in Wellfleet, where you'll find picnic tables, restrooms, supplies, a general store, a bike shop, and free parking.

For more information, contact the Cape Cod Rail Trail at the Massachusetts

Division of State Parks and Recreation, 508/896-3491, www.mass.gov/dem/parks/ccrt.htm. For more information about the Cape Cod National Seashore, contact the National Park Service, 99 Marconi Station Site Road, Wellfleet, MA 02667, 508/349-3785, www.nps.gov/caco.

Options

To extend this trip with a scenic spur trip from the Cape Cod National Seashore Salt Pond Visitor Center at Mile 17.5, turn right (east) on the Seashore bike trail, following it through the woods, across the bridge, and through the marsh until it ends at the old Coast Guard station on the seashore. You'll find beach access, lots of bike parking, restrooms, and outdoor showers.

Locals' Tip: Along the Cape Cod Rail Trail, you'll pass many opportunities for ice cream, hot dogs, and other snacks, but among the best is Arnold's (3580 State Highway/MA-6, Eastham, MA 02642, 508/255-2575, www.arnoldsrestaurant.com). The trail runs past the parking lot, about 15 miles into the ride, which hosts air-conditioned restrooms and minigolf. The restaurant offers a full-service lobster and clam bar, and there's excellent homemade ice cream at the outdoor windows and picnic tables.

Places to Stay: The Ocean Park Inn (3900 MA-6, Eastham, MA 02642, 508/255-1132, www.capecodopi.com) is a no-frills, affordable roadside hotel near the midpoint of the Cape Cod Rail Trail, just minutes from the trail. It offers bike parking and a pool. If you have a roof rack for your bikes, don't trust the overhead clearance signs on the front entrance, however—park by the street and bring your bikes into the main lot on their own.

Driving Directions

From anywhere on Cape Cod, take MA-6 to exit 9 (West Harwich and Dennisport). Drive 0.5 mile on MA-134 South. You will go through two traffic lights. Look carefully for the trailhead sign on the left, just past the Cranberry Square shopping plaza. You'll find a parking lot and trail sign but no facilities here. Bike rentals are available at Barbara's Bike and Sport shop, just past the parking lot. Supplies are available all along MA-134 and along the bike path. Bike shops can be found in Brewster, Eastham, North Eastham, North Harwich, Orleans, South Dennis, and South Wellfleet.

Route Directions

0.0 START at Dennis trailhead.

4.4 Gentle incline on bridge over MA-6.

4.7 *Access point and parking lot at Headwaters Drive on the shore of Hinckleys Pond.*

5.2 *Supplies and ice cream available at Pleasant Lake General Store, with bike racks, picnic tables, and portable toilets.*

8.0 *Access point and parking lot along MA-137 in South Brewster. Picnic tables, bike rentals and shops, restaurants, and ice-cream stands available.*

10.7 *Parking with bike rentals, restaurants, and ice-cream stand.*

11.0 Nickerson State Park. *Free parking, picnic tables, lots of side bike trails, campground, and facilities available.*

12.7 Come off bike path onto town road.

12.8 Turn RIGHT onto West Road, cross bridge over MA-6, and turn LEFT to return to rail trail.

13.7 Cross Main Street, Orleans. *Access point with free parking, supplies, restaurants, ice-cream shops, and Orleans Cycles.*

14.1 Bridge over MA-6. (Beginner riders may want to dismount and walk across the bridge, which has a gentle incline.)

17.1 OPTION: For Cape Cod National Seashore Salt Pond Visitor Center, turn RIGHT onto Locust Road, LEFT onto Salt Pond Road, cross MA-6 with caution at traffic lights, and enter the parking area. *Parking, information, maps, and restrooms available.*

22.0 Arrive at Wellfleet trailhead on LeCount Hollow Road. TURN AROUND and retrace route.

44.0 Return to South Dennis trailhead.

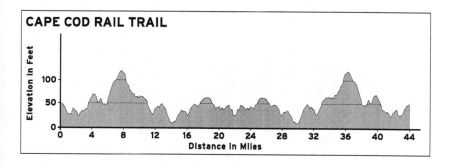

19 PROVINCE LANDS LOOP

BEST (

Provincetown

PAVED BIKE PATH

Difficulty: 3

Total Distance: 8.9 miles

Riding Time: 1-2 hours

Elevation Gain: 260 feet

Summary: A fun ride through a one-of-a-kind town in a spectacular setting.

Even if you've spent your entire life on the coast of Massachusetts, unless it's been in Provincetown, the landscape here will surprise you. It's immediately clear as you drive into town on MA-6. Between the scrub pine and the giant sand dunes, it just doesn't look like any other part of the state's coastline.

And then there's the town itself, and the people who inhabit and visit it, all of which add up to a charismatic spot that's full of surprises. What better way to explore it than on a bike?

Situated at the very tip of Cape Cod, Provincetown traces its roots back to the Mayflower pilgrims. Originally a fishing and whaling town, through the years it's also become known as, among other things, an artists' colony, with a high number of writers and artists living and working there. Notable residents, past and present, include Norman Mailer, Jackson Pollock, and Tennessee Williams. It's also a tourist-friendly town, and on any given day during the summer, the population swells over its year-round numbers.

Before settling down to enjoy some local Wellfleet oysters at a waterfront bar, work up an appetite by pedaling the Province Lands route, which starts at the visitors

You can find people – and bikes – of all kinds in this touristy land's-end town.

center and descends toward Race Point, where you'll find stunningly high sand dunes. Ride through low scrubby pines and bushes in sandy soil, through a low tunnel and a little incline, and toward Herring Cove Beach. The trail comes out at the far end of the parking lot, with seasonal restrooms at the far end. This is a lovely beach, with beach roses and other low-lying shrubs lining the sand dunes.

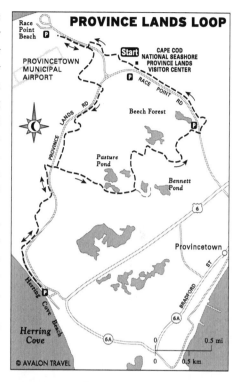

From there you'll ride a steep section followed by a winding downhill past Pasture Pond and into Beech Forest and a totally different ecosystem of trees, swamp, and marshland. On a final short, steep hill, you'll find panoramic views of the dunes and ocean just before you reach the visitors center and the end of the trail.

The Province Lands Visitor Center (daily 9 A.M.–5 P.M., May 1–Oct. 31) offers programs, information, an observation deck, an amphitheater, exhibits, restrooms, a pay phone, a small book and gift store, and trail maps. Parking is free. Restrooms with flush toilets and sinks are available in the parking area year-round. For more information about the Cape Cod National Seashore and the Province Lands Visitor Center, contact the National Park Service, 99 Marconi Station Site Road, Wellfleet, MA 02667, 508/349-3785 or 508/487-1256, www.nps.gov/caco (open May 1–Oct. 31).

Options

This ride can be linked with the Cape Cod Rail Trail. From the Provincelands Visitors Center, head left on Race Point Road and cross MA-6 and MA-6A. Turn left on Commercial Street and then right on 6A/Shore Road. At Mile 7.0, merge with MA-6 and turn right on Castle Road. Castle Road becomes Truro Center Road. Turn right on Depot Road and bear left on Old Country Road. At Mile 14.3, bear left on Bound Brook Island Road and in one 1 mile reach Pole Dike Road; stay straight. Turn left on West Main Street, then bear left on Long Pond Road and cross MA-6. In about 2 miles, turn right at the shore on Ocean View

Drive. In another 2 miles, turn right on Lawrence Road, which becomes LeCount Hollow Road. End at the Cape Cod Rail Trail parking area.

Locals' Tip: Try the Wellfleet oyster shooters—oysters in a shot glass with all the mixings for a Bloody Mary—or any of the other seafood offerings at the Squealing Pig Pub and Oyster Bar (335 Commercial Street, Provincetown, MA 02657, 508/487-5804, www.squealingpigptown.com).

Places to Stay: Stay right downtown in the heart of it at Surfside Hotel and Suites (543 Commercial Street, Provincetown, MA 02657, 508/487-1726, www .surfsideinn.cc).

Driving Directions

From anywhere on Cape Cod, take MA-6 toward Provincetown. You'll pass the intersection with MA-6A. Drive 1.5 miles farther and turn right at the traffic light onto Race Point Road. You'll see signs for Province Lands Visitor Center. Drive 1.4 miles and arrive at the visitors center and parking area. Supplies and bike shops are available in Provincetown.

Route Directions

0.0 START at the trailhead in front of the visitor center.

0.5 Cross the road and come to a T junction. Go RIGHT.

0.9 Arrive at Race Point Beach parking area. *Restrooms available. There is a $3 beach entrance fee for bicyclists.* TURN AROUND.

3.0 Turn RIGHT at intersection toward Herring Cove.

4.1 Arrive at Herring Cove Beach parking area. *Restrooms available. There is a $3 beach entrance fee for bicyclists.* TURN AROUND.

5.3 Continue STRAIGHT at intersection toward Beech Forest.

6.1 *Optional 0.5-mile side trip to Bennett Pond.*

7.4 Arrive at Beech Forest parking lot. *Picnic area and restrooms available.* Turn LEFT, following signs for Province Lands Visitor Center, and cross Race Point Road to continue on bike path.

8.9 END at visitors center parking lot and trailhead.

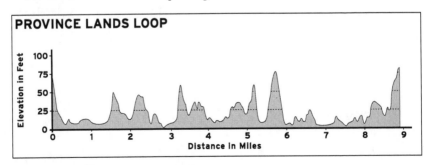

www.moon.com

DESTINATIONS | ACTIVITIES | BLOGS | MAPS | BOOKS

MOON.COM is ready to help plan your next trip! Filled with fresh trip ideas and strategies, author interviews, informative travel blogs, a detailed map library, and descriptions of all the Moon guidebooks, Moon.com is all you need to get out and explore the world—or even places in your own backyard. While at Moon.com, sign up for our monthly e-newsletter for updates on new releases, travel tips, and expert advice from our on-the-go Moon authors. As always, when you travel with Moon, expect an experience that is uncommon and truly unique.

MOON IS ON FACEBOOK—BECOME A FAN!
JOIN THE MOON PHOTO GROUP ON FLICKR

 **OUTDOORS**

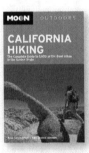

"Well written, thoroughly researched, and packed full of useful information and advice. These guides really do get you into the outdoors."

—GORP.COM

MOON MASSACHUSETTS BIKING

Avalon Travel
a member of the Perseus Books Group
1700 Fourth Street
Berkeley, CA 94710, USA
www.moon.com

Editors: Naomi Adler Dancis, Elizabeth Hansen,
    Sabrina Young
Series Manager: Sabrina Young
Copy Editor: Teresa Elsey
Graphics Coordinator: Elizabeth Jang
Production Coordinator: Elizabeth Jang
Cover Designer: Elizabeth Jang
Interior Designer: Darren Alessi
Map Editor: Mike Morgenfeld
Cartographers: Kat Bennett, Brice Ticen,
    Albert Angulo

ISBN-13: 978-1-59880-569-7

Front cover photo: Mount Greylock in the
Berkshire Mountains © Chris Bernard
Title page photo: Wachusett Reservoir
© Chris Bernard

Printed in the United States of America.

ABOUT THE AUTHOR

Chris Bernard

Chris Bernard is a freelance writer and photographer based in southern Maine. Though he's called many far-flung places home, Chris was born and raised in the northeast – and he always seems to return to his roots. So far he's lived in four of the six New England states, and his wife's family lives in the other two, giving him plenty of chances to ride throughout the region. He's spent much of his life on two wheels – as a kid he raced BMX and in college he rode mountain bikes. He now races cyclocross and road bikes. When he's not at his desk, Chris is usually out on his bike, suffering his way up a hill or chasing his dog through muddy woods.

Chris has been a newspaper and magazine journalist and editor, a senior advertising copywriter, and a technical writer. While researching this book, he got rained on, sunburned, muddied, bloodied, scraped, and bruised – and he loved every second of it. He may not be the fastest rider – he's often seen chasing a disappearing pack – but good luck finding someone who enjoys his time on the bike more.